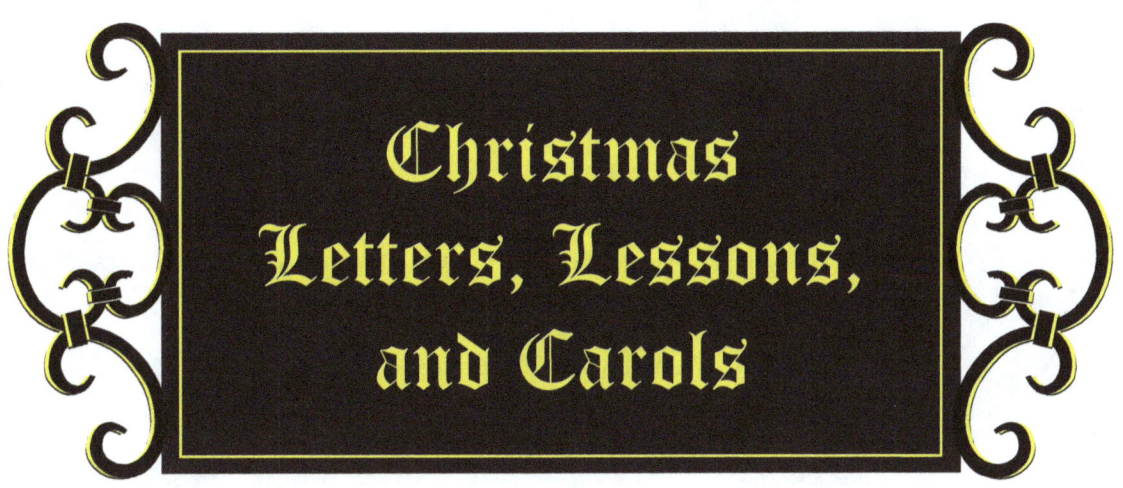

Christmas Letters, Lessons, and Carols

Gordon Kenworthy Reed

"The light shines in the darkness, and the darkness has not overcome it."

John 1:5

© 2017 Gordon Kenworthy Reed

All rights reserved. No part of this book may be
reproduced in any form without written permission from:

Tanglewood Publishing
(800) 241-4016
www.tanglewoodpublishing.org

ISBN: 978-0-9972490-3-3
Printed in the United States of America

Interior design and layout, music notation, and hymn notes by Tammy Williams,
e-mail: turtledoveconsult@gmail.com.

Exterior graphic design/art by Christy Rodriguez.

Acknowledgements

Unless noted otherwise, all carols and hymns printed in this book are in the public domain.

All artwork presented in this book is in the public domain and has been made available for public use through The Metropolitan Museum of Art Open Access Collection, National Gallery of Art Open Access Collection, Web Gallery of Art, ACT (Art in the Christian Tradition) Database, Creative Commons, and Wikimedia Commons.

Dedication

Christmas 1953 was the major turning point in my life. God in His grace and mercy brought Miriam into my life and she is still the best Christmas gift ever 64 years later. So, in praise to Him who gave me her, I gratefully and joyfully dedicate this book to Miriam Elizabeth Clark Reed, the joy and love of my life.

Contents

Preface vii

A Letter, the First Lesson, and a Carol 9
    Christmas: Don't Miss It!

A Letter, the Second Lesson, and a Carol 19
    The Real Christmas Tree I: First Came Adam
    The Real Christmas Tree II: Along Came Noah
    The Real Christmas Tree III: Don't Forget the Women

A Letter, the Third Lesson, and a Carol 49
    The Virgin Mary vs. Women's Lib

A Letter, the Fourth Lesson, and a Carol 61
    Christmas: Enjoy It!

A Letter, the Fifth Lesson, and a Carol 73
    Christmas: Believe It!

A Letter, the Sixth Lesson, and a Carol 87
    We Hear the Christmas Angels I: The Angel of Anticipation
    We Hear the Christmas Angels II: Good News: Gabriel and Mary
    We Hear the Christmas Angels III: Joseph the Dreamer
    We Hear the Christmas Angels IV: "Unto Certain Poor Shepherds"

A Letter, the Seventh Lesson, and a Carol 123
    After the Angels Leave

A Letter, the Eighth Lesson, and a Carol 135
    The Wise Men vs. Secular Humanism

A Letter, the Ninth Lesson, and a Carol 147
    The Sword That Broke Mary's Heart

A Letter, the Tenth Lesson, and a Carol 157
    The Last Christmas Will Last Forever

Hymns and Carols

Angels We have Heard on High	120
As With Gladness Men of Old	144
Gabriel's Message	104
God Rest You Merry, Gentlemen	70
Hail To the Lord's Anointed	46
Hark! the Herald Angels Sing	132
In the Bleak Mid-winter	16
Joy To the World	168
Let All Mortal Flesh Keep Silence	154
Lo, How A Rose e'er Blooming	28
O Come, All Ye Faithful	84
O Come, O Come, Emmanuel	38
O Little Town of Bethlehem	96
Of The Father's Love Begotten	166
Tell Out, My Soul	58
Unto Us A Boy is Born	112

Preface

The title of this book was inspired by the Festival of Nine Lessons and Carols service that has long been associated with King's College Chapel in Cambridge, England. The service originated in 1880 in Truro, Cornwall, where it was held in the small wooden shed that served as the congregation's worship space while the Cathedral of Truro was under construction. Although it appears to have been embraced at that time by the local community, it was not until King's College adopted the service as its own in 1918 that the seeds were sown for its immense growth. It rode a wave a popularity that took on expansive proportions once the College began transmitting live radio broadcasts of the service in 1928. From that point, the Festival of Nine Lessons and Carols rapidly became a tradition in cathedrals, churches, and collegiate chapels of all denominations around the world. The British broadcasts have continued every Christmas Eve since that time, except in 1930. Overseas broadcasts started in the early 1930s, and broadcasts began airing over public radio in the United States in 1979. It continues to be broadcast every Christmas Eve in the United States over National Public Radio. In keeping with 21st century communication modes, it is also broadcast by the BBC via live streaming. It is estimated that there are millions of listeners and viewers worldwide.

The service includes nine scripture readings ("lessons") that recount our fall from grace, the Messianic prophecies, and the Incarnation of Christ. Each reading is followed by a congregational carol or choral anthem that reflects upon the message of the lesson. Aside from local and regional adaptations to reflect cultural and denominational traditions, the format of the service has not changed substantially since 1918.

Regardless of regional variations in the service, its primary theme, as described by Dean Eric Milner-White*, remains the same: "... the development of the loving purposes of God ... [seen] through the windows and the words of the Bible." With the addition of uplifting and thought-provoking pastoral letters from Dr. Reed, the lessons and carols within these pages seek to do the same.

---

* *Eric Milner-White was the dean of King's College who introduced the service in 1918.*

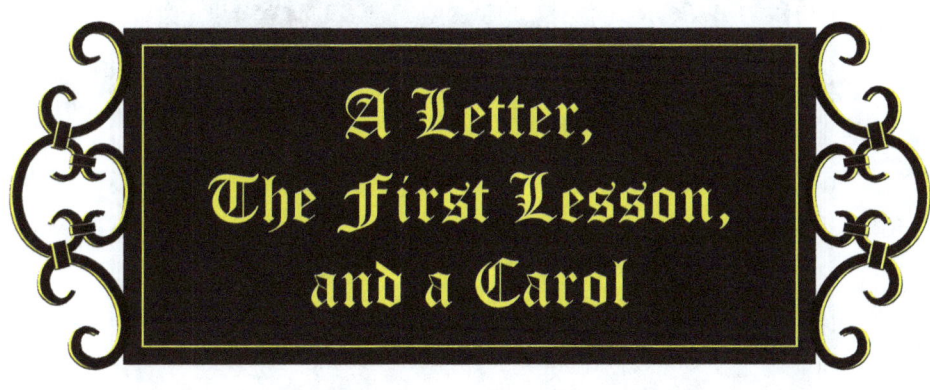

The Nativity (center panel), ca. 1510-15

Gerard David (ca. 1460-1523), Netherlands

Oil on canvas, transferred from wood

The Metropolitan Museum of Art Open Access Collection

This early 16th century work by Gerard David is the center panel of an altarpiece. Following a practice typical of the era, the artist "focuses attention on the mystery of the Incarnation — that is, Christ's birth and sacrifice for the redemption of mankind. Despite the joyful moment depicted, the figures all wear somber expressions, foreshadowing Christ's eventual suffering and sacrifice. The sheaf of grain parallel to the manger refers to John 6:41: 'I am the bread which came down from Heaven.'" (*www.metmuseum.org*)

An altarpiece is a work of art that is placed above and behind the main altar in a Christian church. Altarpieces often consisted of several connecting panels representing key elements of biblical stories.

Christmas Again ... Already?

Dearly Beloved,

Christmas again already? How can twelve months possibly fly by so fast, and how can I possibly be so utterly unprepared again? I guess I'm not so unprepared to celebrate the Savior's birth as I am to celebrate the secular side of Christmas which intrudes itself into this holy day more and more. In fact, as I re-read the old familiar story of Christmas as found in Matthew and Luke, I realize anew how very much the biblical Christmas challenges and rebukes the philosophy embodied in the way the world celebrates its holiday they also call 'Christmas'. Just think for a moment how utterly different the Virgin Mary's outlook on life was from the frantic selfishness of women's lib. Think how differently Joseph looked at life as compared to the modern "macho man." The wise men were the scholars and philosophers of their day. Compare their diligent and humble search for truth to the philosophy of the modern educational establishment as embodied in the propaganda of the NEA. Compare the straightforward efforts of the shepherds to spread the good news of Christ's birth to the spin masters in modern media. Yes, I'm way behind in my present-buying and card-sending and even in decorating (I still don't have my tree), but I'm all charged up and ready to joyfully sing the carols of Christmas, spread the message of Christmas, tell my family and friends how much I love and appreciate them. I long to see the children all dressed up like the angels they are not, and wearing their parents' bathrobes to look like shepherds and wise men as they act out the timeless story of the Savior's birth. Hey, guess what? I'm not at all unprepared for Christmas after all. Bring it on. I can hardly wait.

Much love and many prayers,

Gordon   Miriam

Gordon and Miriam Reed

Christmas: Don't Miss It!

Now the birth of Jesus Christ took place in this way. When his mother Mary had been betrothed to Joseph, before they came together she was found to be with child from the Holy Spirit. ⁹And her husband Joseph, being a just man and unwilling to put her to shame, resolved to divorce her quietly. ²⁰But as he considered these things, behold, an angel of the Lord appeared to him in a dream, saying, "Joseph, son of David, do not fear to take Mary as your wife, for that which is conceived in her is from the Holy Spirit. ²¹She will bear a son, and you shall call his name Jesus, for he will save his people from their sins." ²²All this took place to fulfill what the Lord had spoken by the prophet: ²³"Behold, the virgin shall conceive and bear a son, and they shall call his name Immanuel" (which means, God with us). ²⁴When Joseph woke from sleep, he did as the angel of the Lord commanded him: he took his wife, ²⁵but knew her not until she had given birth to a son. And he called his name Jesus.

- Matthew 1:18-25

೮೨

In those days a decree went out from Caesar Augustus that all the world should be registered. ²This was the first registration when Quirinius was governor of Syria. ³And all went to be registered, each to his own town. ⁴And Joseph also went up from Galilee, from the town of Nazareth, to Judea, to the city of David, which is called Bethlehem, because he was of the house and lineage of David, ⁵to be registered with Mary, his betrothed, who was with child. ⁶And while they were there, the time came for her to give birth. ⁷And she gave birth to her firstborn son and wrapped him in swaddling cloths and laid him in a manger, because there was no place for them in the inn.

- Luke 2:1-7

Christmas has become the most lucrative season of the year for many people. Billions are spent on decorations, gifts, and food. And billions are made. The hype begins in late October or early November, really heats up after Thanksgiving, and becomes a mad frantic rush through the rest of December. It's a much bigger, broader event than it was a few years ago, but there is an alarming blurring going on. The sharp focus has been lost, and Christmas is becoming less and less distinct. Catalogs and stores are filled with Christmas cards but few, if any, mention Christ, and most people seem annoyed or embarrassed if His name is even mentioned, whose birthday we ostensibly are celebrating. (Or is it Santa's birthday?) Some stores forbid their employees from even saying "Merry Christmas," and some now are selling "holiday" trees. The words of the second Psalm come to mind: "He who sits in the heavens shall laugh; the Lord will hold them in derision." The most holy day for believers is accepted in the world only if we are willing to say it is a holiday. In fact, public displays of nativity scenes and any references to Christ have been ruled illegal by many liberal judges who are cowed by the ACLU.

In short, Christmas, which is rushing upon us, is going to pass most people by, and if we're not careful, we too may be swept along without a moment to really ponder these things in our hearts, and with no gift of loving devotion for our dear Savior. What a tragedy! How may we avoid being counted among those of whom it was said, "He came unto His own, and His own received Him not"?

Unfortunately, there's nothing new about all this. From the very beginning of this fabulous story, there have been many who missed the joy and wonder of what happened, and some who almost did. Let's look again and see who missed out on Christmas, who almost did, and why. Then, for a lingering moment see those who did not miss, but found God's greatest gift.

I. Those Who Missed Christmas

The first that comes to mind is, of course, the much maligned inn keeper. By the time Luke interviewed Mary about the birth of Jesus, no one, not even Mary, could remember his name, if she ever knew it. He deserves his reputation. We could excuse him on the basis of his ignorance of who Mary and Joseph really were. But does that excuse a man from helping a poor family like Joseph's? They were so obviously strangers, Mary obviously very pregnant, and both obviously poor and in need of help. Yes, he was a busy man; yes, this was his best chance to make a good profit when people were crowding into the town, willing to pay whatever he asked for a room and meal. What he was doing seemed so important. He was so busy doing what seemed to be so important, that the only really important thing that ever happened to him passed him by.

The world is filled with his like today: materialists who see life only in terms of getting and gaining, and little time for or interest in the poor and needy, the sick and elderly, the lonely and dying. Yes, even Christians get caught up in that attitude if we're not very careful. Do you suppose if the inn keeper had known it would have made a difference? Maybe if he had just stopped for a minute, thought for a moment … but when does a person like that ever really take time to stop or think about anyone other than himself? You never know who that person in need may be.

Another who missed Christmas was Herod, but for entirely different reasons: his guilt and fear and greed for power. Even though he pretended interest when speaking with the Magi — "Go and find this young child, and when you have found Him bring me word again, that I may come and worship Him also" — it was all pretense to mask his evil heart and design.

But the most tragic of all was that the Jewish people as a nation — whose whole purpose for existence was to bring the Messiah into the world — missed Christmas. Their whole long history had been preparation for this grand entrance of their God into His world, and through His people whom he had formed and repeatedly redeemed. But again, there was nothing new in their rejection. Had they not at first rejected Moses? Had they not refused to enter the Promised Land? Had they not stoned and murdered the prophets? Were they not the most bitter enemies of the early Church? So when Christ came into His own land, His own people refused to receive Him.

When I see those who are called by His name today show such disinterest in holy living, serious Bible study, earnest application of Christian truth to their daily lives, I hear again those awful words, "He came unto His own, and His own received Him not."

II. Those Who Almost Missed Christmas

The first was Zacharias, father of John the Baptist. His unbelief brought chastisement on him, and almost cost him even more. Then there was Joseph. When Mary told him of the angel's words and her own pregnancy, his pride and hurt feelings almost cost him the greatest honor any human man has ever been given. But bless him, when God spoke to his heart, he made a decision so profound, so noble, and so right that his name is in the hall of fame of great heroes.

III. Then, Of Course, Some Did Not Miss It at All

1. Mary, with her simple childlike faith and complete submission to God's will.
2. The simple, lowly shepherds who were surprised by wonder and joy.
3. The wise men who would not be deterred by distance or danger, or even their own limited knowledge.
4. Anna and Simeon found Him, too, and departed from this world in peace and great hope, for their eyes saw the Messiah and their hearts rested, safe in the promises fulfilled before their very eyes.

Conclusions: So, the same drama continues today. The mighty and the multitudes continue to miss out on Christmas. They come close. They know the story, but filled with the spirit of the world, frozen by cynicism and unbelief, held in bondage by their own fears, prisoners of greed and pride; they celebrate a Christmas that knows nothing of

Christ and go their own unhappy and empty way towards the grave, gaining the whole world and losing their souls. And, yes, there are some who might miss it if they don't wake up. Like Zacharias, whose understanding of the greatness and faithfulness of God was so limited by his own little formal faith. Or maybe like Joseph, whose manly pride and deeply hurt feelings almost disqualified him to raise God's Son, but who told both God and Mary he was sorry for his sin, and became the real man God called him to be.

Let us be found among those who really and truly find Christmas. Like Mary, and her cousin Elizabeth, yes and even Zacharias and Joseph. Like the busy farmer shepherds, or the seeking, searching wise men. And how do we express this? With joyful worship, with deep and fulfilling meditation on the Incarnation. But even more with glad sharing of the tidings, self-forgetting love for each other and the unloved and unlovable of this world. With gifts of kindness and mercy, and with a deliberate and successful effort to focus on Jesus, His Incarnation, and His call to follow Him in life and death, and into the Father's house above.

In the Bleak Mid-winter

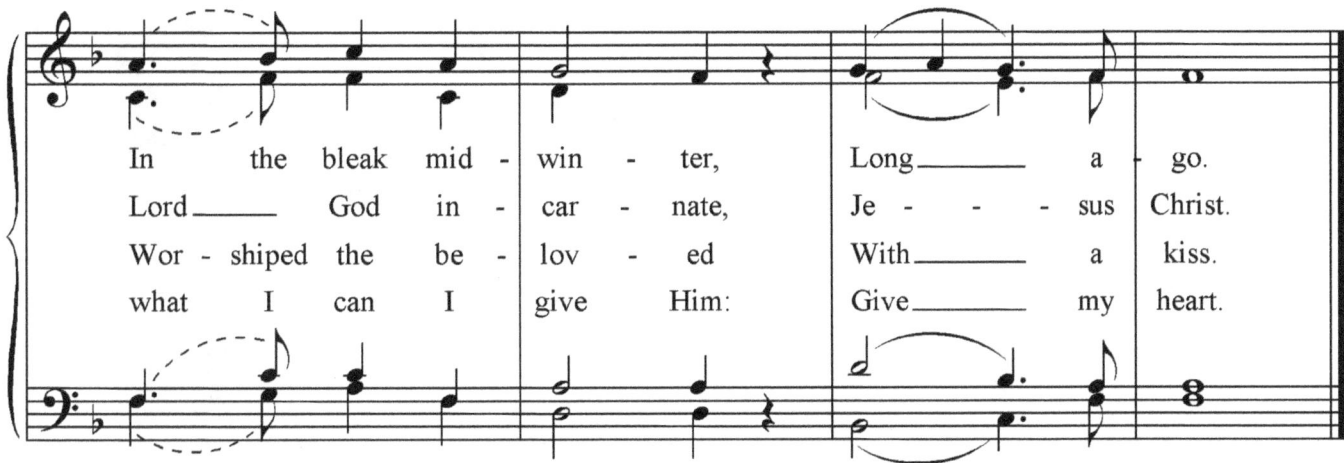

Words: Christina Georgina Rossetti (1830-1894), ca. 1872
Music: Gustav Holst (1874-1934), 1906

Tune: *Cranham*

Hymn Notes

Christina Rossetti was born in London in 1830, the youngest of four children in a family of gifted individuals, all with literary and artistic inclinations. Her father, Gabriele Rossetti, was an Italian poet and political exile who established himself in London as a scholar of Dante, and in 1831 was named chair of the Italian department at King's College. Biographies point to a happy childhood in which the children were read to by their parents, the siblings teamed to produce a family newspaper, sonnet-writing contests were held, and great delight was found in excursions to the family's country cottage. Christina is described as a highly spirited child who worked hard to subdue her temper. The family was involved in the religious politics of the day, and Christina's experiences with such influenced her writing. Her body of poetry is immense and diverse. So respected was her work that, even in her lifetime, debates were sparked as to who was the greatest female poet of the era: Rossetti or Elizabeth Barrett Browning.

In the bleak mid-winter is a gentle but deeply stirring poem that speaks through metaphors and contrasting images, beginning with the backdrop of snow and cold against which Rossetti sets her text. Although Jesus was born in a mild climate, an artistic tradition developed somewhere along the centuries that portrays Him as being born in snowy winter chill. Through her long experience with dreary British winters, Rossetti knew the sense of weariness that bitter cold can bring. So, desiring to create a sense of desolation, she purposely chose to follow tradition and depict Jesus' birth as occurring in the depth of winter. This allowed her to set up a stunning contrast: the Lord of lords, the Light of the World broke into our cold, desolate human darkness, pouring light upon all who would acknowledge Him.

The second stanza points out the paradox between the glorious realm of heaven and the "stable place" that became the birthplace of the King of kings, the Son of God. This theme is not uncommon in Christmas carols, but Rossetti frames it in a such a way that one catches a glimpse of the vastness of eternity and the profundity of the Incarnation. A further contrast occurs in the third stanza, this time between the "throng" of angels and the Incarnate One's humble mother who with quiet reverence "worshiped the beloved with a kiss."

With the words "What can I give Him," the last stanza draws us back to this chapter's lesson. Do you recall the concluding paragraph? "Let us be found among those who really and truly find Christmas. Like Mary, and her cousin Elizabeth, yes and even Zacharias and Joseph. Like the busy farmer shepherds, or the seeking, searching wise men. And how do we express this? With joyful worship, with deep and fulfilling meditation on the Incarnation. But even more with glad sharing of the tidings, self-forgetting love for each other and the unloved and unlovable of this world. With gifts of kindness and mercy, and with a deliberate and successful effort to focus on Jesus, His Incarnation, and His call to follow Him in life and death, and into the Father's house above." The carol summarizes: "Yet what can I give Him: Give my heart."

- TW

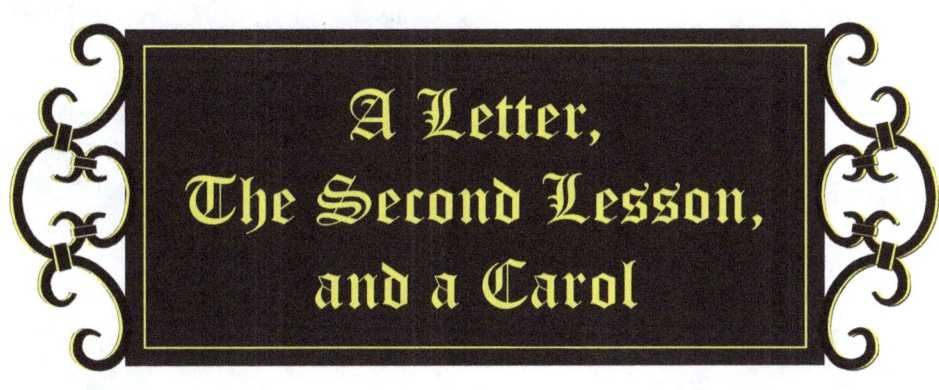

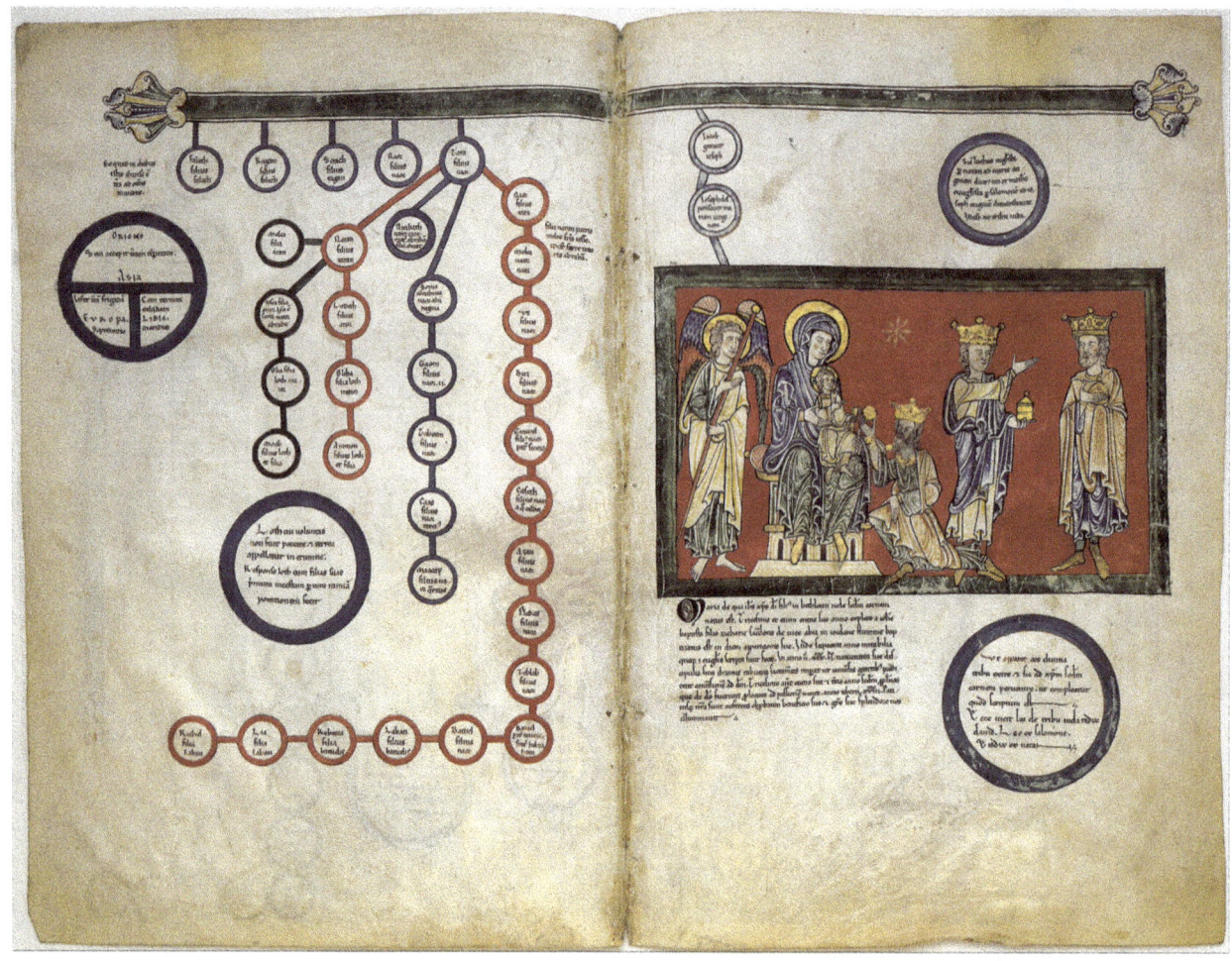

Leaves from a Beatus Manuscript: Bifolium with part of the Genealogy of Christ and the Adoration of the Magi

Spain, ca. 1180

Metropolitan Museum of Art Open Access Collection

Illustrated Beatus manuscripts are derived from commentaries on the Book of Revelation by Beatus of Liébana, an eighth-century Asturian monk and theologian. These manuscripts are unique to medieval Spain and give witness to the academic and artistic abilities within the region's monasteries. The leaf shown above comes from a manuscript disassembled in the 1870s. In their entirety, the pages of this particular manuscript trace the ancestry of Christ from the beginning of the world. The diagram concludes with a portrayal of the magi adoring the Christ Child, who is held by the enthroned Virgin Mary.

Christmas: A Reason to Hope

Dearly Beloved,

Many years ago at Christmas time, I received a phone call from a lady in the congregation I was serving. Her husband was far away on a business trip and not expected home until much later that night. "Pastor," she sobbed, "I just got a phone call from the nursing home my mother-in-law is in. They told me that soon after my father-in-law arrived for his morning visit, she suddenly died. He's there all alone and it will be hours before anyone in the family can get there. Would you please go and stay with him 'til some of us can get there?"

I rushed over as soon as I could and when I went into the room, I found the dear old man sitting by his wife's bed, holding her hand and smiling through his tears. "Mr. Garrett," I said, "I am so sorry your dear wife has passed away." He turned to me with a surprised look on his face, and still smiling he said, "But Pastor, this is what mother and I have been living for all our lives, to go home and be with the Lord."

I was overwhelmed by his quiet confidence and the real joy written on his face. I was also a little ashamed to realize that I didn't measure up to him. I have thought about this many times since, especially at Christmas. The older I get, the more I understand Mr. Garrett's peace and joy, and by God's grace the more I share in it. Christmas is what gives us confidence and even joy when we face the inevitability of death for ourselves and our dear loved ones.

The coming of Christ into the world was the fulfillment of all the prophecies of the Old Testament, and the beginning of the promised new creation. The One who "in the beginning created the heavens and the earth" has also promised to make all things new. Almost all the wonderful prophecies of the coming Messiah include both His first coming as the Lamb of God to save us from our sins, and the return in glory when His eternal Kingdom is brought to reality in the new heavens and the new earth. Many of the best Christmas carols reach beyond his humble birth and speak of the glorious kingdom which he will bring in. None say it better than one of the verses in the familiar carol, "It came upon the midnight clear":

For lo! the days are hastening on by prophet-bard foretold,
when with the ever circling years, comes round the age of gold.

If you ever lose heart and grow doubtful that there will ever be such a wonderful reality, Christmas is God's reminder that all His promises are true and sure. The glory and beauty of our dear Savior's birth reminds us of the greater glory which will surely come. Are you lonely, downcast, and discouraged because of what's going on in your life now? Are you missing your loved ones who have left this world? Look up in hope. Soon, in God's good and appointed time, the Lord and His glorious Kingdom will come! There will be new heavens and a new earth in which righteousness, peace, and joy will be our experience forever. Each Christmas brings us one step closer to the consummation God has promised. You may not be able to dry all your tears now, but like Mr. Garrett, you can smile through your tears and say, "Why this is what we've been living for all our lives!"

May true peace and joy be yours this Christmas and forever more.

Much love and many prayers,

Gordon and Miriam Reed

The Real Christmas Tree 1: First Came Adam and Eve

Then God said, "Let us make man in our image, after our likeness. And let them have dominion over the fish of the sea and over the birds of the heavens and over the livestock and over all the earth and over every creeping thing that creeps on the earth." ²⁷ So God created man in his own image, in the image of God he created him; male and female he created them. ²⁸ And God blessed them. And God said to them, "Be fruitful and multiply and fill the earth and subdue it, and have dominion over the fish of the sea and over the birds of the heavens and over every living thing that moves on the earth." ²⁹ And God said, "Behold, I have given you every plant yielding seed that is on the face of all the earth, and every tree with seed in its fruit. You shall have them for food. ³⁰ And to every beast of the earth and to every bird of the heavens and to everything that creeps on the earth, everything that has the breath of life, I have given every green plant for food." And it was so. ³¹ And God saw everything that he had made, and behold, it was very good. And there was evening and there was morning, the sixth day.

- Genesis 1:26-31

❧

Now the serpent was more crafty than any other beast of the field that the LORD God had made. He said to the woman, "Did God actually say, 'You shall not eat of any tree in the garden'?" ² And the woman said to the serpent, "We may eat of the fruit of the trees in the garden, ³ but God said, 'You shall not eat of the fruit of the tree that is in the midst of the garden, neither shall you touch it, lest you die.'" ⁴ But the serpent said to the woman, "You will not surely die. ⁵ For God knows that when you eat of it your eyes will be opened, and you will be like God, knowing good and evil." ⁶ So when the woman saw that the tree was good for food, and that it was a delight to the eyes, and that the tree was to be desired to make one wise, she took of its fruit and ate, and she also gave some to her husband who was with her, and he ate. ⁷ Then the eyes of both were opened, and they knew that they were naked. And they sewed fig leaves together and made themselves loincloths. ⁸ And they heard the sound of the LORD God walking in the garden in the cool of the day, and the man and his wife hid themselves from the presence of the LORD God among the trees of the garden. ⁹ But the LORD God called to the man and said to him, "Where are you?" ¹⁰ And he said, "I heard the sound of you in the garden, and I was afraid, because I was naked, and I hid myself." ¹¹ He said, "Who told you that you were naked? Have you eaten of the tree of which I commanded you not to eat?" ¹² The man said, "The woman whom you gave to be with me, she gave me fruit of the tree, and I ate." ¹³ Then the LORD God said to the woman, "What is this that you have done?" The woman said, "The serpent deceived me, and I ate." ¹⁴ The LORD God said to the serpent, "Because you have done this, cursed are you above all livestock and above all beasts of the field; on your belly you shall go, and dust you shall eat all the days of your life. ¹⁵ I will put enmity between you and the woman, and between your offspring and her offspring; he shall bruise your head, and you shall bruise his heel."

- Genesis 3:1-15

Where did the custom of having Christmas trees come from? I don't think anyone really knows, but that never seems to inhibit some people from telling you all about it.

I know some folks think having a Christmas tree is a pagan practice, but the grounds on which they say this are not very convincing to me. They point to the practice of ancient pagans who were supposed to have had trees in their homes which were in honor of some imaginary gods and goddesses. Whether or not this really happened, I have no way of knowing. But using this same logic, one could condemn having a blessing before meals or, for that matter, praying at all, for supposedly ancient pagans did both. But who would really argue that Christians should not pray simply because some pagans and other followers of false religions did the same?

However, the sermon today and indeed all the sermons throughout the Advent season about the real Christmas tree have nothing to do with the sort of Christmas tree most of us have in mind. Rather, these messages are about the family tree of our Lord and Savior, Jesus Christ, whose birth we celebrate at Christmas. Humanly speaking, who were His ancestors and what may we learn from considering them that would help us understand more of the meaning of our Savior's birth and His life on earth? Another question of equal importance is: In what way would such a study help us to understand the meaning of our faith and life?

For Matthew, the genealogy of Jesus Christ was one way of proving that He was the true Messiah and, therefore, the true King of the Jews. Thus, Matthew carefully traced the family line of Jesus back through David and all the way to Abraham, the father of the Jewish race. David was the idealized king, and it was to Abraham the promises first came that through his seed all nations of the earth would be blest.

Luke's purpose was to show that Jesus, the Son of Man, had come to seek and save all the lost sheep, both Jew and Gentile. So, Luke traced the lineage all the way back to Adam and Eve to prove the humanity of Jesus and His connection with the human race as a whole. No doubt, Luke was influenced by his many missionary journeys with Paul in which he saw multitudes of Gentiles coming to faith in the Lord Jesus. So, we will follow the line presented by Luke to begin our celebration and understanding of Christmas.

I. Adam and Eve, Created in God's Image

You will never really understand who Jesus Christ is unless and until you understand who Adam was. In fact, you will never truly understand who you are until you understand who Adam was.

Christmas really begins with these words: "So God created man in His own image, in the image of God He created him. Male and female He created them. And the

Lord God formed man from the dust of the ground, and breathed into his nostrils the breath of life."

Adam and Eve were created in God's image to serve under Him as lords and stewards of creation. They were created to reign and at the same time to obey, that they might experience the bliss of intimacy with their Creator; and to discover in ruling over creation and serving under the Creator the full and true meaning of their lives.

Human beings, Adam and Eve, you and me, are like God as no other created beings can possibly be. We alone of all creation, both seen and unseen, bear the image of God. God is personal, self-conscious, creative, ruling the world He made, and good in His nature and in His works. God's image in us means that we have immortal souls which can never die. We are real persons with self-consciousness and with a God-like capacity for knowledge, actions, relationships, and with dominion over the creation. God created bodies for us so that we may express ourselves in this created world, and have the God-given capacity for eternal life. He created us sinless that we might be like Him, holy, happy, and undefiled. God gave Adam and Eve to each other that they might learn through their relationship with each other what it means to have a loving relationship with God Himself. They were placed in a beautiful garden, surrounded by everything they needed to fulfill all their needs and all their legitimate desires. Further, they were given the promise of everlasting life and joy if they acknowledged and obeyed God in all their ways and choices. What a creation! What a prospect! What glorious possibilities and opportunities were theirs to claim. They had but to love, honor, and obey, and they would discover all the joy and fullness of their created purposes. But they had to make choices freely and willingly without coercion, and with the freedom and possibility of failure.

II. Adam and Eve Fallen from Their Glorious Estate and Ruined by the Fall

What happened? You know the story all too well. Our catechism sums up the biblical story of the most terrible tragedy which has ever befallen the human race and is the root of all ills and griefs. The tragic results of their disobedience were far, far worse than they could ever imagine in their worst nightmares. Listen to this brief but brilliant summary from the Westminster Larger Catechism:

> Our first parents, being left to the freedom of their own will, fell from the estate wherein they were created by sinning against God. The sin by which our first parents fell from the estate wherein they were created was their eating of the forbidden fruit. The covenant being made with Adam was not only for

himself, but for his descendants. All mankind descending from him by ordinary generation sinned in him and fell with him in his first transgression. The fall brought mankind into an estate of sin and misery. The sinfulness of that estate where into man fell consists in the guilt of Adam's first sin, the lack of original righteousness, and the corruption of the whole nature which is commonly called original sin, together with all actual transgressions which proceed from it. All mankind, by their fall, lost communion with God, are under His wrath and curse, and so made liable to all miseries in this life, to death itself and the pains of hell forever.

From that moment of rebellion on, everything changed. It changed radically for all creation and all creatures, and for the worse; much, much worse. Not only did their sin bring upon them separation from God, it brought death upon themselves and upon all creation. Instead of being faithful stewards and loving lords of creation, they became tyrants and despoilers of all that God had pronounced good. God did not change, but mankind changed. It wasn't just that Adam and Eve fell from their blessed estate of joy and glory; they became the heads of a fallen race which was doomed to inherit their fallen nature, and doomed to live in a fallen world. Instead of a relationship of love and trust, our first parents hid themselves in unholy fear. Such fear leads to the hatred of the holy and the Holy One. That hatred may take many forms, but always leads to the same inevitable and horrible end, unless grace intervenes.

III. Adam and Eve's Hope

When Adam and Eve fled from God and tried to hide from Him, they did not realize the only safe hiding place from the wrath of God is the wounded heart of God. (Do you know that?) They tried to hide behind the trees of the garden, but there is only one tree where refuge may be found, and that tree is the cross of the Lord Jesus Christ. God found them in their flimsy hiding place, seeking refuge behind flimsy leaves which could not cover their nakedness. He told them of the terrible curse under which they had fallen, and of the fate they had brought upon themselves and upon all creation. But even in the pronouncement of doom, a light broke through the dark clouds and a silver lining of hope was etched against the black sky.

First, God replaced their futile efforts to cover their nakedness with fig leaves by providing animal skins. Thus, the first death to be experienced in creation also suggested something profound about God's mercy. He alone can provide adequate covering for the nakedness of our souls in His holy presence. But an innocent life must be taken to provide covering for the guilty.

God pronounced doom upon Satan for his role in leading Adam and Eve astray. God promised our first parents that Satan's head would be crushed under the heel of the woman's seed: a far-off prophecy of the virgin birth. This is the first promise of the Messiah who would one day come to rescue the fallen race of Adam by crushing the serpent's head. It is also the first indication of the terrible suffering the Messiah would endure to win that battle. "For as in Adam all die, even so in Christ will all be made alive. For since by man came death, by man came also the resurrection of the dead." Just as Adam was the head of a fallen race, so Christ is the head of a redeemed race, a new humanity destined for glory, not condemnation. He whom she would beget would be Eve's true and only hope, and for all who descend from her and Adam by ordinary generation. He alone could atone for their sins and ours. He alone could provide a covering for their guilty nakedness before a holy God.

Yes, that's where it all began. The real Christmas tree points back to the dawn of time and the beginning of the human race. It shows us that our first parents created in God's image fell into sin and misery. They lost paradise and were barred from the tree of life forever … except for that promise which would begin to unfold when the mighty Angel of the Lord came to a young virgin named Mary, a direct descendent of Eve, and told her she would have a baby, not by ordinary generation but by the power of the Holy Spirit she would conceive and bear a Son … the promised Seed of the woman who brings final ruin upon the evil empire of death and hell, and would open anew the gates to Eden and give all God's precious ones to eat of the tree of life in the garden of God.

The promise God made to Eve is the beginning of true hope for all who have inherited the fallen nature of our first parents. God confronts with our fallen nature and the futility of trying to hide from Him. "Where can I go from Your Spirit? Where can I flee from Your presence?" (Psalm 139:7) He calls to us in our foolish hiding places saying, "Where are you?" He seeks us out because that's the kind of God He is. Then, wonder of all wonders, He brings to us the message of salvation, first introduced to our fallen, hopeless, and devastated parents. The Seed of the woman will crush the deceiving serpent's head, and that Holy Seed is none other than our Lord and Savior Jesus Christ, whose birth we begin to celebrate once more.

Lo, How A Rose e'er Blooming

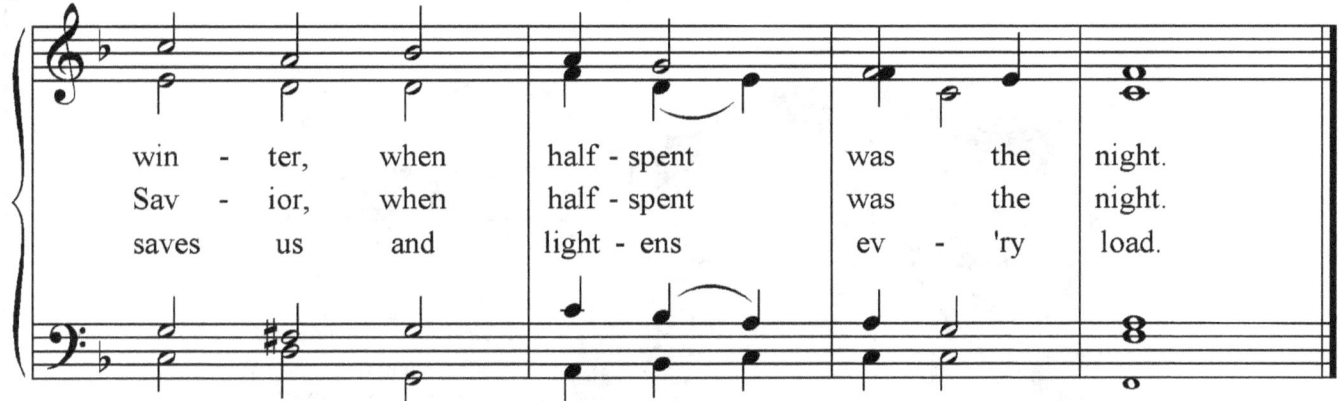

win - ter, when half - spent was the night.	
Sav - ior, when half - spent was the night.	
saves us and light - ens ev - 'ry load.	

Words: Sts. 1-2, 15th century German carol; tr. Theodore Baker (1851-1934), 1894
        St. 3, Friedrich Layritz (1808-1859); tr. Harriet Reynolds Kraugh (1845-1925)
Music: Anonymous, 16th century; arr. Michael Praetorius (1571-1621), 1609

Tune: *Es ist ein ros entsprungen*

Hymn Notes

This anonymous German carol is believed to date back to the early 15th century, although the earliest discovered manuscript containing the text is dated around 1580. Its first known publication occurred in a German hymnal titled *Alte catholische geistliche Kirchengesiinge* (1599). In its original form, the carol contained 23 stanzas. As its source, the text of the first two stanzas draws upon Luke 1-2 and Matthew 2, as well as Isaiah's "stem of Jesse" imagery used in the prophecies recorded in Isaiah 11:1 and 35:1-2. The text also adopts the artistic tradition of casting Jesus' birth "amid the cold of winter." (See notes for *In the bleak mid-winter*, page 17.)

There are two schools of thought regarding the symbolism of the rose as it is used in this hymn. Some scholars believe the original interpretation likely viewed the rose as Mary, the mother of Jesus. This would align with the biblical genealogy of Jesus. It is through this interpretation that the carol came to be - and continues to be - so closely associated with Mary. Michael Praetorius, the influential German composer who wrote the hymn tune's harmonization, offered a different interpretation in 1609: he proposed that the symbolism pointed to Jesus as the rose. That interpretation seems to carry more weight, although the debate continues. In light of that debate, one might find it interesting to note that the original German title, "ein Ros," equates with "ein Reis" in Old German, meaning 'scion', 'sprig', or 'small shoot' - not necessarily a rose.

The English translation of the first and second stanzas are by New York-born Theodore Baker (1851-1934). Baker earned a place in music history as the compiler of *Baker's Biographical Dictionary of Musicians* (first ed. 1900), the first major music reference work that included American composers. His other work spanned a fairly broad swath, ranging from the translation of foreign language hymn texts to conducting one of the first studies of the music of the American Indians.

Of the 23 original stanzas of the hymn, only the first and second won consistent use in denominational hymnals. The oft-used third stanza was written by Friedrich Layritz (1808-1859), a German pastor and musicologist. It incorporates themes from the first chapter of the Gospel of John.

- TW

Tree of Jesse

Bible des Capucins (Champagne, France, ca. 1180)

Tempera and gold leaf on parchment

Wikimedia Commons

The Tree of Jesse became a popular artistic device in religious art in the 12th and 13th centuries. It represents the genealogy of Christ in its depiction of Mary as descended from Jesse, father of King David. The source of the imagery comes from Isaiah 11:1: "And there shall come forth a rod out of the stem of Jesse and a Branch shall grow out of his roots." As in the example here, most renderings show Jesse in a recumbent position with a tree rising from his abdomen. The assorted figures depicted are representative of the lineage of Jesus as documented in Matthew 1:2-16 and Luke 3:23-38.

The Real Christmas Tree 2: Along Came Noah

When man began to multiply on the face of the land and daughters were born to them, [2] the sons of God saw that the daughters of man were attractive. And they took as their wives any they chose. [3] Then the LORD said, "My Spirit shall not abide in man forever, for he is flesh: his days shall be 120 years." [4] The Nephilim were on the earth in those days, and also afterward, when the sons of God came in to the daughters of man and they bore children to them. These were the mighty men who were of old, the men of renown. [5] The LORD saw that the wickedness of man was great in the earth, and that every intention of the thoughts of his heart was only evil continually. [6] And the LORD regretted that he had made man on the earth, and it grieved him to his heart. [7] So the LORD said, "I will blot out man whom I have created from the face of the land, man and animals and creeping things and birds of the heavens, for I am sorry that I have made them." [8] But Noah found favor in the eyes of the LORD. [9] These are the generations of Noah. Noah was a righteous man, blameless in his generation. Noah walked with God. [10] And Noah had three sons, Shem, Ham, and Japheth. [11] Now the earth was corrupt in God's sight, and the earth was filled with violence. [12] And God saw the earth, and behold, it was corrupt, for all flesh had corrupted their way on the earth. [13] And God said to Noah, "I have determined to make an end of all flesh, for the earth is filled with violence through them. Behold, I will destroy them with the earth. [14] Make yourself an ark of gopher wood. Make rooms in the ark, and cover it inside and out with pitch. [15] This is how you are to make it: the length of the ark 300 cubits, its breadth 50 cubits, and its height 30 cubits. [16] Make a roof for the ark, and finish it to a cubit above, and set the door of the ark in its side. Make it with lower, second, and third decks. [17] For behold, I will bring a flood of waters upon the earth to destroy all flesh in which is the breath of life under heaven. Everything that is on the earth shall die. [18] But I will establish my covenant with you, and you shall come into the ark, you, your sons, your wife, and your sons' wives with you. [19] And of every living thing of all flesh, you shall bring two of every sort into the ark to keep them alive with you. They shall be male and female. [20] Of the birds according to their kinds, and of the animals according to their kinds, of every creeping thing of the ground, according to its kind, two of every sort shall come in to you to keep them alive. [21] Also take with you every sort of food that is eaten, and store it up. It shall serve as food for you and for them." [22] Noah did this; he did all that God commanded him.

- Genesis 6:1-22

ೞ

Then God said to Noah and to his sons with him, [9] "Behold, I establish my covenant with you and your offspring after you, [10] and with every living creature that is with you, the birds, the livestock, and every beast of the earth with you, as many as came out of the ark; it is for every beast of the earth. [11] I establish my covenant with you, that never again shall all flesh be cut off by the waters of the flood, and never again shall there be a flood to destroy the earth." [12] And God said, "This is the sign of the covenant that I make between me and you and every living creature that is with you, for all future generations: [13] I have set my bow in the cloud, and it shall be a sign of the covenant between me and the earth. [14] When I bring clouds over the earth and the bow is seen in the clouds, [15] I will remember my covenant that is between me and you and every living creature of all flesh. And the waters shall never again become a flood to destroy all flesh. [16] When the bow is in the clouds, I will see it and remember the everlasting covenant between God and every living creature of all flesh that is on the earth." ¹⁷ God said to Noah, "This is the sign of the covenant that I have established between me and all flesh that is on the earth."

- Genesis 9:8-17

The title of these Christmas messages, "The Real Christmas Tree," may sound strange to most of you, and maybe even heretical to some of you who believe that the Christmas tree is a pagan practice which has no place in the celebration of our Lord's birth. It is not my purpose to condemn or approve the practice of Christmas trees in these sermons, though I do love them. The Christmas tree of which I am speaking is the family tree of Jesus Christ, so far as His earthly ancestors are concerned.

Luke's purpose in relating the genealogy of Jesus was to show His connection with the whole human race, beginning with Adam and Eve. So, he went back beyond the genealogy Matthew gave us, whose purpose was to prove that Jesus Christ, being descended from Abraham, was the true seed of the patriarch and thus heir of the promise that through Abraham's seed all nations would be blest. Of course, Matthew also included David in his genealogy to show that Jesus was the promised Messiah and the true King of Israel. Luke also included David and, for the most part, the two genealogies coincide, though obviously both Matthew and Luke did not include all the generations; just enough to prove the continuity to suit their purposes.

It is truly important for us to know that Jesus was descended from Adam and Eve, for this links Him with all humanity in God's plan of redemption. Our first parents were created in God's own image, that they under His sovereignty might rule over creation. One of the greatest of all the glorious mysteries of our faith meets us at this point. He who created Adam and Eve in His own image became one of their descendants by the Incarnation, when He took upon Himself true human nature and a human body. Thus, the Lord and originator of life submitted to a body of death and, yes, even unto death itself.

When our first parents rebelled against God and rejected His covenant with them, they fell into sin and misery and doomed all their posterity descending from them by ordinary generation to the terrible consequences of their rebellion, including death in this world and eternal separation from God. But God in His mercy came to them in the garden, covered their nakedness, and revealed an incredible hope of future deliverance. One day, the woman's seed would crush the serpent's head, but not without cruel suffering on His part. That day would lie far, far in the future, when One descended from Eve by extraordinary generation — the virgin birth — would come into the world He had created and bear the penalty for their rebellion and ours.

The results of the fall began to manifest themselves right away. Fallen from their original holiness and pristine perfection, Adam and Eve were expelled from paradise and left Eden to live in a sin cursed world. Children were born to them. How many, we do not know, but doubtless a goodly number. Among the first born to them were two sons, Cain and Abel, both with fallen natures like their parents. By faith and grace, Abel was a righteous man, but Cain in jealous rage killed his brother Abel, and the human race began a headlong race towards utter destruction.

After many generations, this brings us to another very significant person in the genealogy of our Lord Jesus Christ: Noah. Had it not been for this godly man, humanly speaking, our Lord Jesus would have never been born. In fact, had it not been for Noah, you never would have been born. For in the time of Noah, the human race had become utterly corrupt. So much so that God pronounced a final judgment on that sinful generation and a catastrophic disruption of all creation. Now consider what was going on in the days of Noah.

I. Noah's World

There is much about the ancient world before the great flood we do not know, but there is much we do know. The Bible in Genesis 6, and in several places in the New Testament, tells us what was happening in the days of Noah. The godly line of Seth, whom God had given to Adam and Eve to replace slain Abel, had all but disappeared from the earth. By the time of Noah, that godly line had been reduced to one man and his family. This was not enough to stem the tide of evil or to stay the hand of God's judgment on the human race. Yes, God seems to always work through a remnant of faithful people, but there comes a time when evil is so overwhelming that nothing can salvage a given culture. This was not only true in Noah's age and place, but the same thing happened in Sodom and Gomorrah and later in all of Canaan. Listen to this discouraging and even frightening description of the moral disintegration of the pre-flood culture, which brought the hand of terrible judgment on the whole earth.

1. The godly line of Seth began to intermarry with unbelievers and produce offspring of wickedness.
2. Tyrannical rulers and governments began to oppress and conquer the weak and defenseless.
3. The resulting culture became totally corrupt and evil.
4. God set a date and hour when He would bring destruction upon the human race and the whole creation by sending a worldwide flood.

Many secular scientists today who know nothing of the physical world before the flood scoff at the idea that such a worldwide catastrophe could possibly happen, and a lot of unthinking and weak-kneed Christians have caved in to this sort of unbelief and suggested, "Well, maybe it was just a flood in the Euphrates valley." Thank God, there has arisen a number of brilliant scientists such as Dr. Henry Morris, former professor of geology and hydrology at Virginia Tech, and, yes, Dr. John Reed, who have made intensive studies which confirm the Genesis account of the flood. Interestingly enough, most of the same secular scientists agree that one day the world will end in fire, but few, if any of them, connect this with the long standing biblical prophecies that God will bring final judgment in the form of fire upon the whole earth.

But the purpose of this sermon is not to prove the case for a worldwide flood, but to show how Noah fits into the family tree of Jesus and thus becomes a vital part of the Christmas story.

II. Noah's Faith and Life in the World, and How He was a Living Prophecy of the Coming of Christ

The first mention of Noah were the words spoken by his father Lamech at the birth of his son whom he named Noah, which means "rest." Obviously, Lamech believed God had a special work for Noah. His words, "This one will comfort us concerning our work and the toil of our hands because of the ground the Lord has cursed," are words of faith and hope. Lamech knew the promise God made to his ancestors, Adam and Eve, that the serpent who had brought such harm to the human race would be defeated by the seed of the woman. I believe Lamech hoped that his son would be that seed. And to a very limited degree he was, in that God thwarted Satan's effort to destroy the human race through Noah and his faith.

The next thing we read about Noah is a natural follow-up of his father's faith and hope: "But Noah found grace in the eyes of the Lord." Everything else we learn about Noah flows out of these words. He was an heir of the covenant and a man saved by grace. But that was not the whole story, nor should it ever be the whole story of one saved by grace. Because he was a man saved by grace, Noah was also "a just man, perfect in his generation, and Noah walked with God." Those were the dimensions of his life, which are infinitely more important than the later dimensions of the ark. This is the pattern of life which should be the story of my life and yours, and of every person who professes Christ. Noah alone of all people on earth in his generation believed the word of God and acted wisely on it. Notice the parallels between Noah and Jesus Christ, and see in his admittedly imperfect life a living prophecy of the coming of Christ.

Noah: "... found grace in the eyes of the Lord."

Jesus: "This is my beloved Son in whom I am well pleased."

Noah: Came into a sinful world under the curse of the fall and under the sentence of judgment. Yet, he lived a godly life, and by his obedience to God's call preached a message of judgment to an unbelieving generation.

Jesus: Came into a sin cursed world under the righteous sentence of judgment and lived a sinless life, proclaimed the word of God, and warned of coming wrath upon those who refused His message of salvation.

Through Noah, a good but fallen man, God gave the human race a second chance. Through Christ, the perfect man, God began a new creation and a new race of humanity, redeemed by grace and destined to live in a future world of perfection and unmingled joy.

Noah: Built an ark for the saving of his family from the flood.

Jesus: Provided escape from eternal condemnation to those who flee to him for salvation.

III. Noah's Reward and Noah's Hope

Because he was the object of God's loving purpose and grace, he was saved from judgment. God revealed to Noah the certainty of the coming flood and how to build an ark for his safety, for the safety of his family, and the preservation of the various species of bird and animal life which with him would inhabit the renewed post-flood world. Noah accepted God's revelation, obeyed his voice, and endured the scorn and rejection of a lost humanity. But when the terrible cataclysm of the deluge wiped out mankind, Noah was borne up on the waters of judgment, safe in the ark of salvation God provided. And when the storms passed, the waters receded, God sent him out with a promise and an assured pattern by which the renewed world would exist until the time of the final end. A rainbow appeared in the sky, sent by God as a sign that never again would the world be destroyed by a flood.

However, soon redeemed Noah became painfully aware of his own imperfections and sinful nature, even as we who are redeemed are brought face to face with our weaknesses and sins. It also became evident that the generations succeeding Noah would demonstrate the same fallen nature which doomed the former generation. Surely, Noah understood that this new beginning was not the full answer to God's promise to Adam and Eve. The serpent's head had not been crushed. This would only take place when afar descendent of Noah appeared on earth whose name is Jesus. He alone could remove the curse placed on creation by the fall. He alone could conquer sin, death, and hell, and bring in a Kingdom which will never end. He closed the yawning gates of hell and opened the gates to Eden once more. He provided an ark of salvation which will endure the fires of final judgment. All that Noah meant to the hopes of the human race in his generation are magnified infinitely in our Lord Jesus Christ.

The days of His first advent on earth are long since past. The day of His return draws nearer and nearer. The frightening similarities between the ancient world of Noah and the world of the twenty-first century are obvious to us all, and on a scale of evil even surpassing the age of Noah. Take heart! For Jesus said, "As it was in the days of Noah, so shall be the coming of the Son of Man …" Scripture tells us that God has already set the day and hour of the end. So I ask you, do you know Him? Are you safely in the ark of grace? Will you live in the new creation of perfection when this old one has passed away?

The manger of the infant Jesus has become the ark of mercy to bear us safely through the fires of judgment. "Come, let us adore Him, Christ the Lord; Messiah Adonai."

O Come, O Come, Emmanuel

Words: Latin, ca. 9th century; tr. John Mason Neale (1818-1866), 1851
Music: Plainsong Mode 1, 15th century

Tune: *Veni Emmanuel*

6. O come, thou Dayspring from on high,
   And cheer us by thy drawing nigh;
   Disperse the gloomy clouds of night,
   And death's dark shadow put to flight.
   Rejoice …

7. O come, Desire of nations,
   Bind in one the hearts of all mankind;
   Bid thou our sad divisions cease,
   And be thyself our King of Peace.
   Rejoice …

8. O come, O come, Emmanuel,
   And ransom captive Israel,
   That mourns in lonely exile here
   Until the Son of God appear. *Rejoice ...*

Hymn Notes

This ancient Advent hymn, one of the oldest Christian hymns to remain in continuous use, originated from a 9th century (or earlier) hymn that was part of the Roman Catholic liturgy. That hymn is known as the *Great 'O' Antiphons*. There is an intentional three-part structure to the hymn. First, each of the original seven stanzas refers to Christ by an Old Testament title, thereby presenting Him as the fulfillment of Old Testament prophecies.

1. Emmanuel ("God With Us") ... Isaiah 7:14
2. Wisdom ... Sirach 24:3, Wisdom 8:1
3. Adonai (Yahweh, Lord; Giver of the Law) ... Exodus 3:2; 6:6; 19:16-20
4. Root of Jesse (Jesus' lineage)... Isaiah 11:1; 53:2, Jeremiah 23:5-6
5. Key of David (Jesus' lineage)... Isaiah 22:22
6. Dayspring (Morning Star) ... Isaiah 14:12, Malachi 4:2
7. Desired One ... Jeremiah 10:7, Isaiah 33:22

The second element of this intentional structure rests in usage. The hymn's seven stanzas were meant to be sung one at a time and in sequential order, one on each day of the week leading up to Christmas.

The third element is a reverse acrostic that is evident in the original Latin but hidden to us in English. The first letter of each of the Latin words for the titles of the Messiah, written backwards, count down the remaining days until Christmas: EROCRAS or "ero cras," meaning "I will be [with you] tomorrow."

Sapientia (Wisdom)
Adonai (Lord)
Radix (Root)
Clavis (Key)
Oriens (Dawn)
Rex (King)
Emmanuel (Emmanuel)*

Originally, the stanza that we now identify as the first was actually the last. — *TW*

Tree of Jesse, ca. 1500

Attributed to Jan Mostaert (ca. 1475-1552), Netherlands

Oil on oak panel

Web Gallery of Art, Wikimedia Commons

This representation of the Tree of Jesse presents a somewhat more literal depiction of Jesus' lineage than the previous example. Upon the tree that is growing from Jesse's body are the twelve Kings of Judah: David (with a harp), Solomon, Rehoboam, Abijah, Asa, Jehoshaphat, Jehoram, Uzziah, Jotham, Ahaz, Hezekiah, and Manasseh. Mary is seated in the tree's crown with the Christ Child in her lap, surrounded by angels. The figures positioned on either side of Jesse are believed to be the prophets Isaiah and Jeremiah. The figure in white, kneeling in the left foreground, is a nun. She is thought to be the donor of the painting. It was common practice during the Middle Ages and Renaissance for artists to incorporate the portraits of benefactors into their paintings.

The Real Christmas Tree 3: Don't Forget the Women

The book of the genealogy of Jesus Christ, the son of David, the son of Abraham. ²Abraham was the father of Isaac, and Isaac the father of Jacob, and Jacob the father of Judah and his brothers, ³and Judah the father of Perez and Zerah by Tamar, and Perez the father of Hezron, and Hezron the father of Ram, ⁴and Ram the father of Amminadab, and Amminadab the father of Nahshon, and Nahshon the father of Salmon, ⁵and Salmon the father of Boaz by Rahab, and Boaz the father of Obed by Ruth, and Obed the father of Jesse, ⁶and Jesse the father of David the king. And David was the father of Solomon by the wife of Uriah, ⁷and Solomon the father of Rehoboam, and Rehoboam the father of Abijah, and Abijah the father of Asaph, ⁸and Asaph the father of Jehoshaphat, and Jehoshaphat the father of Joram, and Joram the father of Uzziah, ⁹and Uzziah the father of Jotham, and Jotham the father of Ahaz, and Ahaz the father of Hezekiah, ¹⁰and Hezekiah the father of Manasseh, and Manasseh the father of Amos, and Amos the father of Josiah, ¹¹and Josiah the father of Jechoniah and his brothers, at the time of the deportation to Babylon. ¹²And after the deportation to Babylon: Jechoniah was the father of Shealtiel, and Shealtiel the father of Zerubbabel, ¹³and Zerubbabel the father of Abiud, and Abiud the father of Eliakim, and Eliakim the father of Azor, ¹⁴and Azor the father of Zadok, and Zadok the father of Achim, and Achim the father of Eliud, ¹⁵and Eliud the father of Eleazar, and Eleazar the father of Matthan, and Matthan the father of Jacob, ¹⁶and Jacob the father of Joseph the husband of Mary, of whom Jesus was born, who is called Christ. ¹⁷So all the generations from Abraham to David were fourteen generations, and from David to the deportation to Babylon fourteen generations, and from the deportation to Babylon to the Christ fourteen generations.

— Matthew 1:1-17

The family tree of our Lord Jesus has some very unusual branches! When Matthew, the Jewish historian, traced the genealogy of Jesus, he mentioned the names of five women in this long list of "begots." Let me read just these few lines from Matthew 1:

"Judah begot Perez and Zerah by Tamar. Salmon begot Boaz by Rahab. Boaz begot Obed by Ruth. David begot Solomon by her who had been the wife of Uriah. Jacob begot Joseph the husband of Mary of whom was born Jesus who is called Christ."

In all the forty-two generations included in his genealogy, Matthew mentions but five women. You have to ask, why in the world would a Jewish historian even think of including women in a genealogy which typically goes from father to son? What is even more strange, almost bizarre, are the five he chose by the inspiration of the Holy Spirit. Why did he not mention Abraham's wife, Sarah, or Rachel, or Rebecca, or maybe the mothers of good kings like Jehoshaphat, Hezekiah, or Josiah?

I think there are some wonderful truths wrapped up under the real Christmas tree - the family tree of our Lord. And none of these truths are more precious, instructive, or heartwarming than these truths discovered in the stories of these five women: Tamar, Rahab, Ruth, Bathsheba, and Mary. Three blatantly immoral women, one dusky skinned foreigner, and one peasant girl who became pregnant before her marriage. We must ask ourselves not only why these five deserve special mention above the many virtuous women who might have been mentioned, but what lessons the Holy Spirit would have us learn. Let me suggest at least four of these lessons to be understood.

I. God's Sovereignty in Election is According to Grace and Not Works

Just on the surface of things, there is not one of these five women on the list of our Lord's ancestors that any one of us would have chosen to be in the genealogy of our Lord. In fact, we probably would have conveniently omitted their names if it had been up to us. Like all of Christ's ancestors, they were sinners to be sure, but such sinners as you and I would avoid having any association with at all.

When our Lord was on earth, He was severely criticized and even condemned for having any fellowship at all with this sort, for it was said of Him, "This man receives sinners and dines with them." While eating in the home of Simon the Pharisee, a sinful woman came into the place they were eating and poured costly perfume on His feet, kissing them and washing them with her tears. Simon was outraged and shocked that Jesus allowed her to do this, but the Lord rebuked Simon and forgave the woman her sinful past. Luke records the names of three women who ministered to Christ, and observed that "Jesus had healed them of evil spirits and infirmities."

But God's election is not according to human wisdom or human righteousness. Did not the apostle Paul write: "You see your calling brethren, that not many were wise according to the flesh, not many mighty, not many noble are called. But God has chosen the foolish things of this world to put to shame the wise, and God has chosen the weak things of the world to put to shame the mighty; and the base things of this world, and things which are despised, God has chosen ... that no flesh should glory in His presence."

Remember this, beloved, that the gap between the worst sinners of this world and the best and most righteous is far, far less than the gap between the holiest person in all the world and God. But our merciful God is so great that He takes the worst people who ever lived and turns them into saints and messengers of His grace. He adopts people into His family that you would never and have never even invited to church. Yes, God's election is always according to grace and not human standing or even good works.

II. God's Election is Not Only unto Salvation but unto Righteousness; That is, the Grace which Saves also Transforms

We have no idea what happened in the life of Tamar after the disgraceful incident which led to her pregnancy by her father-in-law, Judah. We are not told what happened to her or even what sort of person she became, but she and one of the sons she bore are in the line of the Christ.

We know much more about Rahab the harlot. She learned of the God of Israel, repented of her sin, and cast her lot with Israel at the threat of her life. She looked to God in faith and was saved, and married a man of Israel. Thus, she is included in the favored list. In Hebrews 11, she is cited as a hero of faith.

As for Ruth the Moabite girl, she left her native land and came into Israel to be with her widowed mother-in-law. There she demonstrated that she, too, had turned in faith to Israel's God. In time, she married an Israelite, Boaz, who became the great-grandfather of David the King, and so she was, of course, David's great-grandmother.

The story of Bathsheba is all too familiar. She was the wife of one of David's most valiant and loyal warriors. But David looked on her, wanted her, took her, and arranged for Uriah to be killed in battle. Amazing grace, God spared both David and Bathsheba, and after being forgiven, David made her his wife by whom was born Solomon, and through whom our Lord came.

As for Mary, she is the one bright light of faith, godliness, and submission to God's will we find among the five women mentioned here. In the eyes of the world, she was no better than the other four, and maybe worse. For the true account of her pregnancy was never accepted by unbelievers then or now.

It is very important for us to draw a fine line at this point. We must always be open to and seeking the lost for Christ, especially those whose lives are in disgrace and ruin because of sin. And the message we proclaim to them is the message of Jesus to the woman taken in the very act adultery: "Neither do I condemn thee, go and sin no more." For if we omit the first part, we leave people without hope. If we omit the second part, we leave them with false hope. The grace which justifies is instantaneous and forever. The grace which transforms is a process never-ending in this life.

III. Never Underestimate What God Can Do In and Through a Person's Life, Including Your Own

If for no other reason, these people are included in Jesus' genealogy as a lesson to each one of us about ourselves and about other people, too. You may think that you are insignificant and unimportant simply because you're not a missionary, a minister, an elder or deacon, or Sunday school teacher, or because you're not rich or famous. Most of us in the final sense are no more nor less than a very small link in a very long chain. What names of those present today will be known even in Christ's Church a hundred years from now? From time to time, God raises up an Abraham, a Moses, a David or Daniel, a Paul or Peter, but for the most part, our place is small and our purpose simple: keep the faith and pass it on. Live for Christ now, and die in His grace. But never for one minute forget that you are so important in God's eyes that He sent His Son to save you. Just living daily for Christ, repenting of sin, and persevering may not sound exciting, but if we do this by God's grace, we will have fulfilled our purpose and mission in life.

Maybe your problem is not that you think yourself to be unimportant, but that you think others are, or at least that they are much less important than you and unfit for your company in or out of church. Hear again the lesson God taught Simon Peter on top of the house of Simon the Tanner in the city of Joppa. While Peter was waiting for the meal to be served, he fell asleep and had a dream. In that dream, he saw a sheet let down from heaven filled with all manner of animals, clean and unclean according to the dietary laws of the Jews. He heard a voice from heaven saying, "Arise Peter, kill and eat." Peter's response was that he had never eaten anything unclean. "What God has cleansed, call not common or unclean," the voice said. This was God's rebuke and His preparation to send Peter to the home of an "unclean" Gentile to bring the news of salvation.

When will we ever learn the same lesson? When will we ever stop looking down on people because of their background, or race, or status in society and regarding them as "common and unclean" and unfit for our company?

IV. Finally We See the Depths of Christ's Humiliation and the Wonder of His Amazing Grace

How wonderful to know that our Lord was willing to so completely identify with our lost and helpless estate. The book of Philippians spells out the story in these words: "Who being in the form of God did not consider it robbery to be equal with God, but made Himself of no reputation, taking the form of a bondservant, and coming in the likeness of men. And being found in appearance as a man, He humbled Himself and became obedient unto death, even the death of the cross." And in Galatians we read: "God sent forth His Son, born of a woman, born under the law to redeem those who were under the law."

But it is precisely this willing humility which assures our salvation and delivers us from the curse of sin and death. If we only found "good people" in Christ's genealogy, we might conclude that He came to save only "good people," and, unfortunately, a lot of Christians seem to believe this. But it was to the fallen and lost that Christ came. And such were we. He came to save us from death and hell, and to lift us from our helpless and hopeless estate. Most of us are at best nobodies in the eyes of the world and by its standards. But in God's eyes and heart, even the smallest and weakest of sinners is of such infinite worth that He gave His beloved and only begotten Son to be our Savior. And wonder of wonders, God knows that one day you will not only be with Him in glory, you will be like Him, the image of God fully restored in all He has redeemed. And when you are there, among the many in that countless throng you will meet with the likes of Tamar, Rahab, Ruth, Bathsheba, and of course Mary. In many ways, these five women are among the most beautiful branches of the real Christmas tree, the family tree of our Lord Jesus, for they assure us that we, too, will eat of the tree of life which grows in the garden of God, called heaven.

Hail To the Lord's Anointed

Words: James Montgomery (1771-1854), 1821; paraphrase of Psalm 72
Music: Traditional German melody, 17th century
Tune: *Es flog ein kleins Waldvögelein*

4. Kings shall bow down before him,
   And gold and incense bring;
   All nations shall adore him,
   His praise all people sing;
   To him shall prayer unceasing
   And daily vows ascend;
   His kingdom still increasing,
   A kingdom without end.

5. O'er every foe victorious,
   He on his throne shall rest;
   From age to age more glorious,
   All blessing and all blest:
   The tide of time shall never
   His covenant remove;
   His Name shall stand for ever,
   His changeless Name of Love.

Hymn Notes

Hymnals tend to use only three or four of the original eight stanzas of this paraphrase of Psalm 72. It was written by Scottish-born James Montgomery in 1821. Montgomery felt that he was born to be a poet, but circumstances led him down a long, frustrating path before he found his niche.

At the tender age of seven, he was sent to seminary to begin training for the ministry. It was there that he began writing poetry and set a goal to write two volumes in the style of John Milton. He was not the best of students and was dismissed at the age of 16 to begin an apprenticeship at a bakery. Although unhappy in the position, he remained for a year and a half, after which he accepted a similar position in another town. He soon gave that up and, determined to achieve his dream, packed his few belongings and moved to London, certain that he would find a publisher for his poems. It was not to be. He survived on odd jobs until 1792 when, at age 21, he became assistant to a Mr. Gales, a bookseller and printer of the *Sheffield Register*. Apparently, Mr. Gales possessed strong political convictions and was not afraid to express them. Fleeing prosecution for his outspoken rebellion, he left England in 1794, giving charge of the newspaper to Montgomery. With that, Montgomery finally found his niche and remained as editor of the newly-named *Sheffield Iris* for 32 years.

A strong Abolitionist, Montgomery was not hesitant to stand up for his beliefs and was imprisoned on two occasions for newspaper reporting that was not appreciated by the ruling political establishment.

The long desired publication of his poetry came in 1797 with the release of *Prison Amusements*, written during one of his prison terms. It was the first of twelve collections of poetry, three volumes of hymns, and assorted lectures that would be published.

Montgomery's family belonged to the Moravian Church. He strayed away in his youth, but found his way back at the age of 43, became an avid worker for missions, and was readmitted to the Moravian congregation. At the time, he expressed his feelings as follows:

> People of the living God,
> I have sought the world around,
> Paths of sin and sorrow trod,
> Peace and comfort nowhere found.
> Now to you my spirit turns —
> Turns a fugitive unblest,
> Brethren, where your altar burns,
> O receive me into rest.

- TW

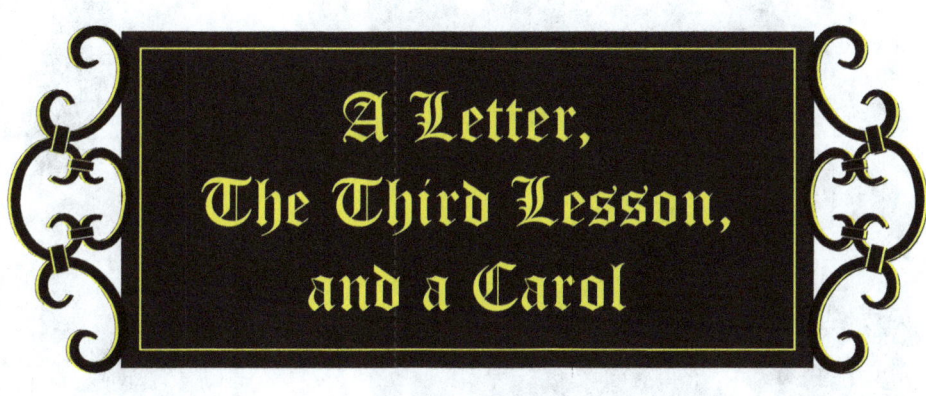

Archangel Gabriel: The Virgin Annunciate, ca. 1510

Gerard David (ca. 1455-1523), Netherlands

Oil on oak panel

The Metropolitan Museum of Art Open Access Collection

"These two panels, along with the depictions of the Passion that decorated their reverses, originally formed the movable wings of an altarpiece. When the wings were closed, the Archangel Gabriel and the Virgin Annunciate were shown. When opened, on certain feast days, the Christ Carrying the Cross and the Resurrection would have been displayed, flanking a central image, perhaps the Lamentation."

(*www.metmuseum.org*)

Christmas 2013

Dearly Beloved,

Can you believe it? Here we are ... it's Christmas time again. Nothing can dim or drive away the joy we share as believers in the wonder and glory of our Savior's birth. But the world and the devil sure are trying hard to rob us of joy and peace on earth. In many distressing ways, they've done a pretty good job of trying. Although the good news of our Lord is being proclaimed throughout the earth and in almost every nation of the world, there is at least some limited exposure to the Gospel; still there are many disappointments, sorrows, and setbacks for believers.

In so many places in the world, Christians are hated, despised, and persecuted. Not a few live and witness for Christ at great personal danger. But this is nothing new. The story of Christmas began in a background of hardship and danger. The nation in which Jesus was born had been conquered by the Romans, who ruled with an iron hand and a wooden cross for all who opposed them.

Young Mary was no doubt exposed to gossip and slander, and was in a position to be stoned to death. Just as the time came for her baby to be born, she was forced to make a long and difficult journey to be enrolled for taxation, along with her husband, Joseph. Her delivery room was a barn. His cradle was a manger. When the puppet king Herod heard of His birth, he tried his best to murder Him. To save His life, Joseph and Mary fled into exile in Egypt, far from Herod's wrath and reach.

After a fairly uneventful childhood, Jesus would enter into the ministry for which His Father sent Him into the world. He was hated, ridiculed, opposed, and slandered by many every step of the way. In the end, He was fully despised and rejected, tried, tortured, and crucified. This pattern has been worked out in the lives of His followers from that time to this. Yes, there have been some glorious victories, but most often only by heroic effort of brave martyrs willing to follow in His footsteps.

So, don't be disheartened because of all the suffering and hatred being inflicted on the suffering body of Christ. We celebrate a victory, not a defeat or an illusion. The Father has appointed the day and the hour when Christ will return in power and glory to conquer all His and our enemies, and to bring to fulfillment the promised kingdom of glory and peace. More and more, I realize that this hope is really what Christmas is all about. So: "Rejoice in glorious hope, our Lord, the Judge shall come and take His servants up to their eternal home. Lift up your heart, lift up your voice! Rejoice, again I say, rejoice!" *("Rejoice! The Lord is King," Charles Wesley, 1746)*

        With love and appreciation for you and all yours.
        May you have a blessed Christmas and a glorious forever,

        Gordon and Miriam Reed

The Virgin Mary vs. Women's Lib

In the sixth month, the angel Gabriel was sent from God to a city of Galilee named Nazareth [27] to a virgin betrothed to a man whose name was Joseph, of the house of David. And the virgin's name was Mary. [28] And he came to her and said, "Greetings, O favored one, the Lord is with you!" [29] But she was greatly troubled at the saying, and tried to discern what sort of greeting this might be. [30] And the angel said to her, "Do not be afraid, Mary, for you have found favor with God. [31] And behold, you will conceive in your womb and bear a son, and you shall call his name Jesus. [32] He will be great and will be called the Son of the Most High. And the Lord God will give to him the throne of his father David, [33] and he will reign over the house of Jacob forever, and of his kingdom there will be no end." [34] And Mary said to the angel, "How will this be, since I am a virgin?" [35] And the angel answered her, "The Holy Spirit will come upon you, and the power of the Most High will overshadow you; therefore the child to be born will be called holy — the Son of God. [36] And behold, your relative Elizabeth in her old age has also conceived a son, and this is the sixth month with her who was called barren. [37] For nothing will be impossible with God." [38] And Mary said, "Behold, I am the servant of the Lord; let it be to me according to your word." And the angel departed from her. ... [46] And Mary said, "My soul magnifies the Lord, [47] and my spirit rejoices in God my Savior, [48] for he has looked on the humble estate of his servant. For behold, from now on all generations will call me blessed; [49] for he who is mighty has done great things for me, and holy is his name. [50] And his mercy is for those who fear him from generation to generation. [51] He has shown strength with his arm; he has scattered the proud in the thoughts of their hearts; [52] he has brought down the mighty from their thrones and exalted those of humble estate; [53] he has filled the hungry with good things, and the rich he has sent away empty. [54] He has helped his servant Israel, in remembrance of his mercy, [55] as he spoke to our fathers, to Abraham and to his offspring forever."

- Luke 1:26-38; 46-55

When Joseph and Mary took the infant Jesus to the temple to fulfill the requirements of the law on His behalf, they were met by an old man named Simeon who had been assured by God that he would not die until he saw the Messiah. When he saw the Holy Infant, he took Him in his arms and blessed God that the promise had been fulfilled. He also said, "This child is destined for the fall and rising of many in Israel, and for a sign which shall be spoken against." Among other things, this meant that Jesus would be the occasion for great controversy, and would challenge the prevailing attitudes and values which were popular then and now. Simeon's prophecy was and continues to be fulfilled down to this very day. The coming of Jesus into the world challenges the value systems and the ideas which dominate the minds of most people. This becomes very clear when we read of the story of the angel Gabriel's visit to the Virgin Mary and her remarkable response to his startling news of her impending pregnancy.

This is going to be painful and annoying to some of you, and maybe even make you very angry. But hear me out and, even more important, listen to these scriptures with a mind and heart open to what the Holy Spirit will say. Dear friends, wake up. Christianity is no longer the dominant culture in this dear land of ours. We are a counterculture, and a thorn in the flesh of the current secular culture which dominates our own country and so much of the world. You and your faith and life values will never be accepted or even admired by the world. And any attempt on our part to address such issues of indecency and immodesty or even the sacredness of human life is regarded as an effort on our part to impose our religious values on other people. The people who make such charges are themselves furiously at work to impose their non-values on our culture and into the minds of our people.

I. Mary's Situation Before the Visit of Gabriel

Our introduction to Mary begins with these simple words in Matthew: "Now the birth of Jesus Christ was as follows: After His mother Mary was betrothed to Joseph, before they came together, she was found with child of the Holy Spirit." Then later, Luke spells out more of the details in his narrative: "Now in the sixth month [of Elizabeth's pregnancy], the angel Gabriel was sent by God to a virgin named Mary who was betrothed to a man named Joseph." We know very little more about her. According to Jewish custom, she would have been in her teen years. We know she was, like Joseph, probably descended from King David. We know also that her lineage, though carefully traced, did not ensure her of any wealth or standing in her time. Most likely, she was of a lowly but pious family who eagerly awaited the coming of the Messiah, and like all good Jews prayed daily for His coming.

If Mary was a typical teenager of her time and place, she was probably doing her assigned chores, cleaning house, or watching after the young children. (She would not have been hanging out at the mall or texting a friend while she was driving at 70 mph.) Perhaps this visit from Gabriel came as she was deeply engaged in prayer and meditation on God's Word. And I suppose like most of us, young and old, she was most likely committed, on the surface at least, to doing God's will. Her life was calm, predictable, and pretty much routine. She knew she would soon be married to a good, steady, reliable, and probably somewhat dull man a good many years her senior.

II. The Unexpected Visitor Who Turned Her Life Upside Down

Then came a bombshell in the form of God's angel with the most startling, upsetting, and wildly unimaginable announcement possible. She was hailed by the angel in these words: "Rejoice highly favored one, the Lord is with you; blessed are you among women."

In the big picture, Mary was an absolute nobody. Sure, she was descended from David, and so were thousands of others like her. (Believe it or not, according to a well worked-out genealogy, I am descended from Charlemagne, but I have no plans to go to Paris and claim the throne of France. In the first place, I would be committed to a funny farm for even suggesting it.)

Mary knew her life was insignificant and mundane, so why did God send the highest angel in Heaven to greet her, and why did he say these things? She was scared; plenty scared, and wondered what this was all about.

Then, Gabriel quieted her fears and began to explain that at long last the Messiah would shortly come, and come in this way. She would conceive and bear a son and call His name Jesus. He would be great, called the Son of the Highest, and God would give Him the throne of His ancestor David. He would reign over that kingdom for ever, and His kingdom would never end.

It's one thing to pray for the Messiah to come; it's another thing to be told He would come to her, and in this way. Mary asked the natural question: "How can this possibly be since I am a virgin?" The answer was that the Holy Spirit would come upon her, and that which would be conceived in her would be the Son of God!

Her life was no longer calm, peaceful, and predictable. It was now turned upside down, was dangerous and unpredictable, and all her plans for marriage and for happiness and fulfillment had just been thrown out the window.

III. Mary's Choices

Though it is not said in so many words, I believe Mary had a choice. She could either accept or reject the will of God for her life. She found herself facing the same choice which Queen Esther had to make many years before. Esther was given a choice: to play her part in God's plan of redemption, or to choose safety, pleasure, and happiness. She was also told that if she refused, God would use another, but her life would have no meaning and she would ultimately lose everything.

Now Mary had to either accept or reject her God-given role. She knew this would mean an end to her plans and her self interests and happiness. Neither Joseph nor any other man would ever have her. She would most likely be publicly disgraced, and could even lose her life according to Jewish law. No one — not even her fiancé, her family, her friends, or any of her neighbors — would ever believe anything but the worst of her.

She could refuse the call, never tell a soul about the visit from Gabriel, and go on her way, carrying out her own plans, living her life according to her own wishes, and finding fulfillment and happiness her own way. After all, it was her body the angel was talking about, and didn't she have the right to decide what to do about this unexpected pregnancy? Which is exactly the choice many people must make — even those who claim to be Christians.

Dear Christian daughters and sisters, you, too, have to face the same basic issues. You are surrounded by a world that has totally different values from the word of God. You are pressured on every side, as never before, to conform to the world's values. Little do we realize how much we are influenced even by such movements in this world which we reject on the surface. These pressures affect every aspect of your life, from what you wear (or don't wear); to what you say; to your attitude towards your marriage, your children, your parents, your house, your time, and, above all, your priorities. What are you teaching your children about what's really important in their lives? Deep down in your heart, if you had to choose, would you rather your child be a great social success, succeed in career, and have a beautiful home and all the other good things, or would you rather that beloved child truly love Jesus with all her/his heart and put Him ahead of all these other things? Mary's and your choice comes down to the same thing: "To whom do I truly belong, and who will I serve in life — God or mammon?"

IV. Mary's Commitment

Facing all these issues, Mary's words from her heart are absolutely incredible. "Be it unto me according to your word." Most women would and do respond, "Be it unto me according to my own wishes and the popular opinions of the world." Mary knew, as you must learn sometimes by bitter experience, you can't have it both ways. In the end, it will be either, "Be it unto me according to your word" or "Be it unto me according to my desires." Now do you understand Simeon's warning to Mary? "This child is set for the fall and rising of many, and a sign which will be spoken against. Yea and a sword will pierce through your own heart also."

Your choices, even made this very day, will identify you as nothing else and will affect for good or ill your life, and your husband, and your children, and their children yet to be born for many generations to come. Don't be deceived, daughters of Eve; what Satan wants for you is not happiness and fulfillment, which he promises. He wants to ensnare and trap you and make you his servant by telling you the road to happiness lies in disobeying God and following your own instincts and desires. Yes, there is grief and pain on the roads of this life, but compare the grief and age-long consequences of Eve's choice to the willingness of Mary to accept the Lord's will for her life. Pain and grief she surely knew, too, but what a gift she gave to the world, and what eternal happiness and praise belong to her. Truly, in the words of Elizabeth, she was "blest among women." And let Mary's words be your words and your heart commitment to the Lord Jesus: "Be it unto me according to your word." And, "My soul does magnify the Lord, and my soul has rejoiced in God my Savior. For He has regarded the lowly state of His maidservant. For behold, henceforth all generations shall call me blessed."

Thank you, dear mother of mine in heaven, for making those choices long ago. Thank you, dear wife of mine, for the same, and even more so. Thank you, dear daughters of mine, for walking that same path. Thank you, dear daughters and sisters in the faith, for the beautiful contrast between you and the women of the world. And thank you, dear Lord Jesus, for saying to the Father for my salvation, "Not my will, but Thine be done." Which was another way of saying what your mother Mary once said, "Be it unto me, according to your word."

What an example and what a challenge the Virgin Mary presents to Christian women in this fading, crumbling culture of ours. And not just to the women, but to all of us who worship her Son as Savior and Lord. No, we do not worship Mary, but we honor her as our sister in the Lord, and as a worthy role model to challenge our culture with ideals and values that come from above.

Tell Out, My Soul

Words: Timothy Dudley-Smith (b. 1926), 1961; based on Luke 1:46-55
Music: Walter Greatorex (1877-1949), 1919

Tune: *Woodlands*

Words Copyright © 1962, Renewal 1990 Hope Publishing Company, Carol Stream, IL 60188.
All rights reserved. Used by permission.

Hymn Notes

This exuberant paraphrase of Luke 1:46-55 expresses the joy of Mary's song of praise as recorded in that passage. First published in 1965, it was one of the first hymns written by Timothy Dudley-Smith and deemed to be his best known. Of the text, he wrote in 1984:

> I did not think of myself . . . as having in any way the gifts of a hymn-writer when in May 1961 I jotted down a set of verses, beginning "Tell out, my soul, the greatness of the Lord." I was reading a review copy of the New English Bible New Testament, in which that line appears exactly as I have put it above; I saw in it the first line of a poem, and speedily wrote the rest.

Dudley-Smith was born in 1926 in Manchester, England. After 30 years of service as a priest in the Anglican Church, he became Bishop of Thetford in 1981. He has been living in retirement since 1992. As a hymn writer, Dudley-Smith has published approximately 400 texts which have appeared in various collections. Many of his hymns appear in hymnals throughout the English-speaking world and in translation. He is an honorary vice-president of the Hymn Society of Great Britain and Ireland, a Fellow of the Hymn Society in the United States and Canada, and a Fellow of the Royal School of Church Music. In 2003, he was awarded an OBE (Order of the British Empire) 'for services to hymnody', and in 2009 an honorary Doctor of Divinity (DD) from the University of Durham (England).

The tune *Woodlands* was composed by Walter Greatorex in 1919 for use with the hymn *Lift up your hearts*. Forty-six years later, it was chosen to be paired with *Tell out, my soul.* It is the hymn tune for which he is best remembered. Greatorex was an English composer and musician who had the youthful distinction of being a boy chorister at King's College, Cambridge. His education continued at Derby School and St. John's College, Cambridge. The hymn *Lift up your hearts* - paired with Greatorex's tune *Woodlands* - became the Derby School hymn. In 1900, he was appointed an assistant music master at Uppingham School, and in 1911 became Director of Music at Gresham's School, where he remained until his retirement in 1949.

Greatorex composed other hymns and organ music. He has the noted distinction of having taught the renowned composers Benjamin Britten and Lennox Berkeley, and the English-American poet W.H. Auden.

- TW

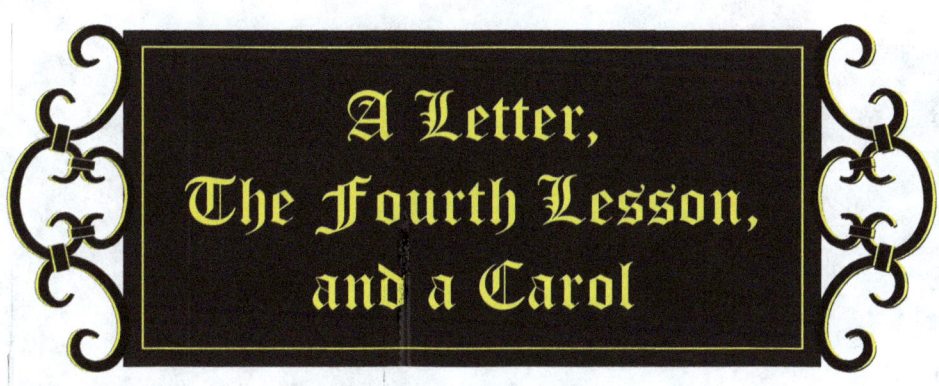

Visitation of Mary to Elizabeth, ca. 1528

Jacopo da Pontormo (1494-1556), Italy

Oil on wood

Web Gallery of Art and ACT Database

This depiction of Mary's visit to her cousin, Elizabeth (mother of John the Baptist), after her encounter with the angel Gabriel portrays the deep affection between the two women. The movement of the fabric of their clothing, contrasted against the stillness of the background, might suggest the joy that both experienced in the wake of the momentous revelations they had so recently received. That joy is addressed in this chapter.

Christmas Joy

Dearly Beloved,

The thing which is most amazing to me about Christmas is the way God did it, and the people He used to make it happen. Just for a moment, forget the trappings of Christmas as a holiday and think only of the Incarnation. God the Creator was preparing to enter the world He made, by becoming a man. The Creator was about to become a creature also. That is the basic and central fact of the Incarnation.

The question is, "How will He do it?" Let any mere mortal write the script for this greatest of all dramas, and it would inevitably come out entirely different from the Christmas story we know and love so well. It would be spectacular, and probably bombastic in the extreme. It would be a combination of the coronation of the world's mightiest monarch, the lighting of the Olympic flame, the World Series, the Super Bowl, and the Macy's Thanksgiving Day Parade. It would be announced, broadcast, and televised with all the pomp and ceremony beyond imagination.

But that's not how God did it. The ancient prophets had foreseen His coming without fully understanding what they had foreseen. When the time came for this greatest of all events since creation, the only announcement was an angelic visit to a little peasant maiden named Mary, and later to her fiancé-husband, and they were absolutely nobodies! It gets even better. The earthly human body of the mighty Creator God at its beginning was almost microscopic. After He was conceived in the womb of the virgin girl by the power of the Holy Spirit, that infant body developed as any other baby (don't call an unborn child a fetus!) would develop.

About the time for Mary to deliver, Joseph her husband took her along with him to Bethlehem to register for the coming census for the purpose of taxation. (Governments haven't changed much, have they?) There in the very lowliest of circumstances, in a cattle stall, in a manger, God became man. That's how He did it. So, we may hear the words, "Fear not, for behold I bring you good tidings of great joy which shall be to all people," and believe they are both true and meant for us.

We, too, may identify with people like Mary and Joseph and the shepherds. They were people just like us — nobodies in the eyes of the world, lowly and without fame or recognition. Yet it was to such people, then and now, God came to bring life, hope, love, and joy. Amazing, isn't it? God knows who I am. God cares about the likes of you and me. God came seeking and saving lost sinners, like us. The story so simple is so true, indeed it is truth!

    I like the way God did it, don't you?

With lots of love,

Gordon and Miriam Reed

Christmas: Enjoy It!

A Christmas Communion Meditation

Now after Jesus was born in Bethlehem of Judea in the days of Herod the king, behold, wise men from the east came to Jerusalem, [2] saying, "Where is he who has been born king of the Jews? For we saw his star when it rose and have come to worship him." [3] When Herod the king heard this, he was troubled, and all Jerusalem with him; [4] and assembling all the chief priests and scribes of the people, he inquired of them where the Christ was to be born. [5] They told him, "In Bethlehem of Judea, for so it is written by the prophet: [6] "'And you, O Bethlehem, in the land of Judah, are by no means least among the rulers of Judah; for from you shall come a ruler who will shepherd my people Israel.'" [7] Then Herod summoned the wise men secretly and ascertained from them what time the star had appeared. [8] And he sent them to Bethlehem, saying, "Go and search diligently for the child, and when you have found him, bring me word, that I too may come and worship him." [9] After listening to the king, they went on their way. And behold, the star that they had seen when it rose went before them until it came to rest over the place where the child was. [10] When they saw the star, they rejoiced exceedingly with great joy. [11] And going into the house, they saw the child with Mary his mother, and they fell down and worshiped him. Then, opening their treasures, they offered him gifts, gold and frankincense and myrrh. [12] And being warned in a dream not to return to Herod, they departed to their own country by another way.

- Matthew 2:1-12

Yes, I know the world has tried to steal Christmas. It has secularized it as a holiday, refusing to say 'Christmas', let alone 'Jesus Christ'. The celebration of the birth of our Savior has even been outlawed and criminalized in much of our society. The facts of Christmas are ridiculed, sometimes even within the organized Church. We're not sure whether to be outraged, scandalized, or driven to tears.

Well, I for one plan to do what I've been doing since infancy … enjoy Christmas! Enjoy it to the fullest extent because that's what God means for us to do. You don't believe me? Just travel back in time to the first Christmas and I'll show you from Scripture that Christmas is meant to be enjoyed.

And who were the first folk to enjoy Christmas? Two women and an unborn baby. After the angel Gabriel had visited Mary with the startling announcement that she was to conceive by the Holy Spirit and bear the Messiah, she made a journey to see her cousin Elizabeth, who was in the sixth month of her own very unusual pregnancy. When Mary entered the house, Elizabeth, who was not a Presbyterian of course, shouted for joy, praising God for the baby Mary would birth. In the midst of her holy mirth, she said to Mary, "For indeed, as soon as the voice of your greeting sounded in my ears, the babe leaped for joy in my womb." So, even little unborn John rejoiced in the news Mary brought. How perfect! The first person to really enjoy Christmas was a little child, a very little child. (And Elizabeth got a kick out of it, too!)

Both shepherds and wise men rejoiced when they heard the news. So it seems that, biblically, God intends for us to have "exceeding great joy" when we hear and celebrate the "good tidings of great joy." Maybe if we discover the reason for their joy of old, we will have our joy ... maybe our lost joy restored.

I. The Joy of Elizabeth, Mary, and John

Why was Elizabeth so ecstatic when Mary came for her visit? Her ecstasy was also communicated to the baby she was carrying, or was it the other way around? There was no mystery about their joy. Let Elizabeth speak for herself. She will tell us why she was so happy and why her baby "leaped for joy." An angel of God had told her husband that their baby would be the herald of Messiah's coming. So, when Mary came to her home and greeted her, Elizabeth was filled with the Holy Spirit, who revealed that Mary was pregnant with the Messiah. It was all true! God's promises were being fulfilled, and the presence of Mary and the Baby she was carrying were confirmation. Elizabeth praised God that Mary had believed the angel's words to her, and at long last the plan of the ages was being unfolded before her very eyes. As for the unborn John, his joy was an instinct of praise and wonder. Later on in his life, Christ would be the only joy he would ever know, for his life was a burden of hardship cut short by Herod's wicked sword. But for now, the presence of the Lord and His servant brought joy, and still does, even for those whose lives are filled with heartache and sorrow.

Joy is always contagious. (If only Christians understood that!) Mary picked up on that spreading joy and sang a song of joy. And what does that song tell us about Mary's joy? "My spirit rejoiced in God, my Savior ... He has done great things for me and holy is His name. His mercy is great ..." If we can say those same things — and all believers can and should — then ours, too, is a joy that transcends all circumstances of woe or well-being. Since you know that God in Christ is your Savior and has done great things for you, you may join Elizabeth, John, and Mary in their joyful celebration.

II. The Joy of the Shepherds

When the Angel of the Lord appeared to the shepherds, they were scared out of their wits, as well they should have been. But in response to their fright, the angel said, "Fear not for I bring you good tidings of GREAT JOY!" This revelation was not a time for fear, but an occasion of great joy! And what news did the angel bring that demanded a response of great joy? "For unto you is born this day in the city of David, a Savior, who is Christ the Lord." Now that's a whole mouthful of joy. Unwrap it carefully, and don't miss a single word. "Unto YOU." God's great gift is always personal. He sent His Son to die for you. Know this, dear child of God, you are the object of God's eternal love, the recipient of His greatest gift. What great value the Father placed on your soul.

Note again: "This day." The gift of God is not only personal; it is always in the present tense. Remember some of the wonderful presents of yesteryear? I can't remember what happened to my big red wagon, or my wind-up train and tractor, or even my yellow corduroy shirt and red bow tie when I was the hottest teenager in the west side of Weaverville. They live as relics of my childhood and youth, but only on the shelf of memory. But the best of all gifts never fades nor wears out. The shepherds had heard for years the Messiah would come some day, but all of a sudden, "one day" became today, and remains forever in the glorious present tense.

And the gift itself? "A Savior, Messiah Adonai." "The gift of God is eternal life through Jesus Christ our Lord." A personal, present gift is also a very, very precious gift. A Savior, the one thing I've always longed for, even when I didn't know it.

Tell us, O shepherds, did you enjoy Christmas? "Enjoy it? Our joy knew no bounds. We went everywhere, glorifying and praising God for what we had seen and heard."

Their joy, like that of Elizabeth's, Mary's, and John's was focused on one thing: God's great gift of a Savior. What is your joy focused on this Christmas? Do you see what they saw? Do you hear what they heard? God has sent His Son into a fallen world to redeem sinners and raise them from despair and death. Joy? Oh, yes! But only those who truly understand that apart from God's grace there is no hope, no reason for joy, will experience the true joy of Christmas.

III. The Joy of the Wise Men

"When they saw the star, they rejoiced with exceeding great joy … and they fell down and worshiped the young Child." They had traveled far to find what they sought. They were guided by a star, but even more, no doubt, by the writings of the Hebrew prophets which Daniel had brought into their land and to their ancestors long years before. Have you ever read those same promises of hope? Have you read those powerful, beautiful words from Isaiah and the other prophets? Of course you have, and were moved to the very depths of your being by the wonder and beauty of what they foretold. So, when at last these seeking men of old were led to believe the time had come for the fulfillment of the promises of a Redeemer, a light to the Gentiles, they set out to find Him. Theirs was the incredible, impossible journey. Where were they going? How would they find the way? How would they know if they had found the right person? No answers ... just believing, trusting, and following a mysterious star. Naturally, they came at last to Jerusalem, the city of the great King David. But from there, they were sent by the scribes and crafty, evil Herod to Bethlehem. Still following the star, they went. At last the star stopped; right over the place where the holy family now lived. Their search was over. They found Him of whom the prophets had written. They found a little boy, just a little tot, just a peasant's child. But they rejoiced with exceeding great joy as they presented their gifts of gold, frankincense, and myrrh. (In some countries of the ancient world, by law gifts of gold and costly perfumes could only be given to royalty or offered to gods.) There was so much they did not understand as they knelt before Him, but they did believe they had found the promised Savior. Their joy of giving their costly gifts was overwhelmed by greater joy of a greater gift they received from God.

IV. Your Joy

And now we have walked where these saints of old have walked. We have heard with our ears what they heard. Our eyes of faith have beheld what and Whom they saw, and so much more, for we have seen the cross and the empty tomb. And like them, we await once more His glorious appearing. Christmas? "Rejoice with exceeding great joy," and go to your homes, your loved ones, and your precious memories this Christmas Eve, and enjoy Christmas to the fullest, richest measure, and enjoy it forever, for now we have a Savior, Messiah Adonai, Christ the Lord. Through Him and Him alone, the gift of God is eternal life. Accept it, understand its meaning, and join all the holy throng above and here on earth as you rejoice with exceeding great joy.

God Rest You Merry, Gentlemen

Words: Traditional English carol, 18th century
Music: Traditional English melody, 18th century

Tune: *God Rest You Merry*

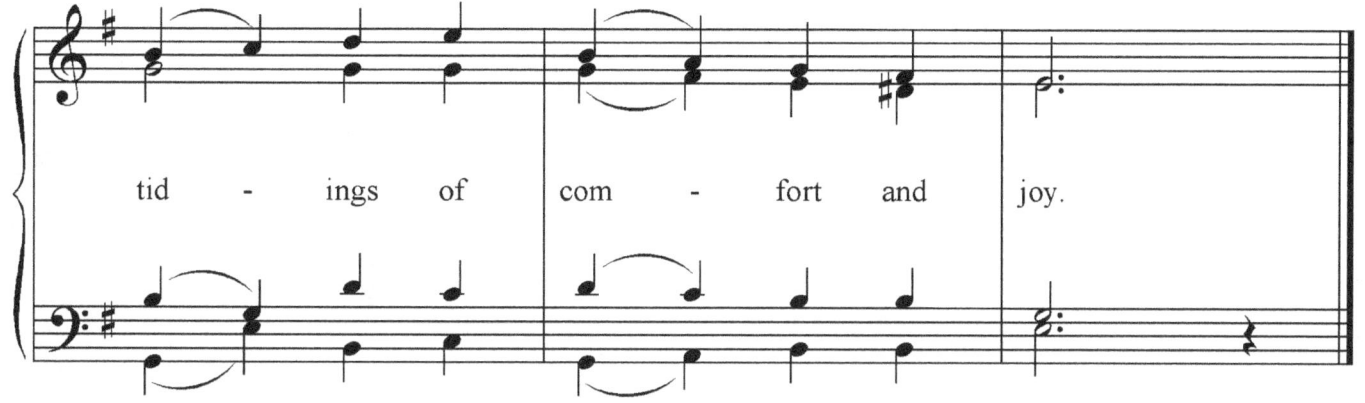

tid - ings of com - fort and joy.

4. "Fear not," then said the angel,
"Let nothing you affright;
This day is born a Savior,
Of a pure virgin bright,
To free all those who trust in him
From Satan's pow'r and might." *Refrain*

5. The shepherds at those tidings,
Rejoicéd much in mind,
And left their flocks a-feeding,
In tempest, storm, and wind,
And went to Bethlehem straightway,
This blessed babe to find: *Refrain*

6. But when to Bethlehem they came,
Whereas this infant lay,
They found him in a manger,
Where oxen feed on hay;
His mother Mary kneeling,
Unto the Lord did pray: *Refrain*

7. With sudden joy and gladness
The shepherds were beguiled,
To see the Babe of Israel
Before His mother mild.
O then with joy and cheerfulness
Rejoice, each mother's child. *Refrain*

8. Now to the Lord sing praises,
All you within this place,
And with true love and brotherhood
Each other now embrace;
This holy tide of Christmas,
Doth bring redeeming grace. *Refrain*

* *Jewry - land of the Israelites*

Hymn Notes

The precise origins of *God rest ye merry, gentlemen* are unknown, but it is believed to have been sung as early as the 15th century by singing bands that traveled around London from tavern to tavern. There is evidence, too, that it was sung by town watchmen to earn extra money during the Christmas season by caroling along the streets. The carol's first known publication occurred in 1833 in *Christmas Carols Ancient and Modern*, a collection of seasonal carols gathered by William B. Sandys.

Because language has changed so much in the past 500 years, it is important to the understanding of this carol that we look at the actual meaning of its opening phrase. In the 15th century, *merry* meant 'strong' or 'mighty'. *Rest* meant to 'keep' or 'make'. Notice, too, the proper placement of the comma in that first phrase. The opening line, then, actually means, "God make you mighty, gentlemen."

During the period when this carol is believed to have developed, church music consisted primarily of Latin chant sung almost exclusively by choir and clergy, giving little opportunity for church-goers to express their faith through song. In response, the people found satisfaction in composing their own religious songs for singing in gatherings outside of church. The songs were joyful, melodic, and written in the vernacular language. *God rest ye merry, gentlemen* is thought to be one such carol.
- *TW*

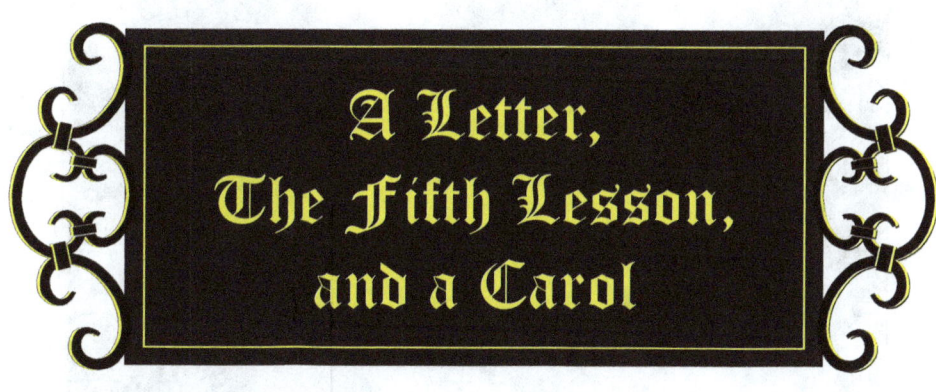

The Annunciation, 1672

Luca Giordano (1634-1705), Italy

Oil on canvas

The Metropolitan Museum of Art Open Access Collection

This is another example of an altarpiece. Luca Giordano, one of the leading painters in Naples in the late 17th century, painted it after a trip to Venice. Note the lily gently grasped in Gabriel's hand. The white lily, a symbol of purity and piety, is used in Christian art as a motif for the Virgin Mary.

It's Okay to Cry at Christmas

Dearly Beloved,

It's okay to cry at Christmas. Many years ago, just two days before Christmas, a young woman lay in her bed weeping uncontrollably. This last incident that devastated her so might seem so trivial it was hardly worth a single tear, but wait before you make rash judgment on her and listen to her story. You may find yourself crying with her.

In many ways, her life had been one tragedy after another, with only a relatively few happy days to remember. While still a very little girl, just starting second grade, her mother died suddenly at the age of 29. For her grief-stricken father, this was the second wife he had lost to early death. Because his work carried him far from home, his daughter went to live with her favorite aunt. But that was not a very happy time, for her uncle by marriage was a scoundrel and stole the little girl's meager heritage from her dead mother. And, within two more years, this aunt, her foster mother, died, too. Then her father became ill, and after a lingering illness he died. This made three parents she had lost in six years. Again, she went to live with another aunt who was good to her, and whose husband also was as a second father. However, her sorrow at the death of her dear parents still haunted her. She felt as if she really didn't belong to anyone.

She finished high school and college before she reached the age of twenty, and then went to work supporting herself and still longing for a family of her own, which she thought she would never have. Life went on for several more years, until one summer she went to visit the aunt who had taken her in after her parents and foster mother had died. There was a handsome young man in that town, just back from the war in Europe, who caught her eye and whose eyes bugged wide open when he saw her. Within a few months, they were married.

At long last, it seemed that life was going to be much better, and it was. Soon, they were expecting their first child and she could hardly wait for the coming birth. Tragedy struck again and the little boy, perfectly formed and beautiful, died in the trauma of birth. She had never known such grief as this. But before long she was pregnant again, and this time a sweet little girl was born alive and healthy, to be followed in the next few years by three more children. Life was good again. Her husband's business was growing and prospering. They built a new home. He was elected to the city council, and all was well. Then dark clouds once more closed in on her life. The Great Depression that devastated this country in the 1930s wiped out their business almost overnight. Soon, the new house had to go and, on top of that, just after moving into a dingy little two-room apartment with four children, she discovered she was pregnant once more. It got worse. As the Depression deepened, her husband could find no work and they were forced to sell many of their possessions to buy food and pay rent.

Shortly after the fifth and last baby was born, her husband found work — a thousand miles away from home! There was no choice; he had to go or the family would starve. He was gone almost two years. From his meager salary, he was able to send home a little money and even baskets of food from time to time. The story is almost over. In that dismal time, a few days before Christmas, he sent her the usual monthly check for the bare necessities of life, and from that pittance she managed to save back seven dollar bills to provide a meager Christmas for her children. Then once more, like the straw that broke the camel's back, tragedy struck. She was only out of the room for a few moments, but while she was gone, the baby boy, now a little over two years, found the pretty pieces of paper lying on the table, managed to drag them down, and merrily tossed them into the open grate fire. When she came back into the room, she saw the last of her Christmas dinner and her hopes go up in smoke. It was too much. This was the low point of a very sad life. It couldn't get any worse. All night she wept and prayed and longed for her husband, but sleep would not come. Finally, at daybreak she arose wearily from her bed to face the day before Christmas with little hope and no joy at all. It would take a miracle even to have a meal on Christmas Day. Still, she prayed. When the mailman came that last day before Christmas, she found a letter from her best friend from college days, whom she had not seen for years. (That friend's name was Miriam, but not the one you know.) She opened the letter, and the miracle happened. Inside the note was a crisp new ten-dollar bill and a wish for a merry Christmas. Later that day, a box of toys came from the same dear friend.

There were many long hard years ahead, but in spite of everything, Christmas was very special that year, and before the next one rolled around, her husband found work in the town where they lived and life slowly improved in every way. She had many years to enjoy life and the family God had given her. You see, the young woman was my dear mother, and the baby boy who tried to ruin her Christmas was me. Yes, my mother cried all night just before Christmas Eve, as she had many times before and after, but that was okay. She had plenty of reasons for her tears. I am confident she will never cry again, for she is with the Lord who said He would wipe away every tear from her eyes, and He has done just that.

Many of you who read this during this Christmas season have plenty of reasons for tears, too. God has never told us not to cry, just that one day He will wipe away all our tears. What tears were shed in Bethlehem that terrible day when Herod's butchers killed all the little baby boys from two years old and under, a tragedy difficult to even imagine. Listen to the lament in Matthew's Gospel as he quoted from Jeremiah the prophet: "A voice was heard in Ramah, lamentation, weeping, and great mourning, Rachel weeping for her children, refusing to be comforted because they are no more."

But the path our Savior would walk in His short life was tear-strewn, too. Despised and forsaken, betrayed and abused, tortured and finally killed, Jesus wept. He wept when His best friend died. He wept when He saw the people of Jerusalem reject Him and seal their own fate. He wept in the bitter garden of Gethsemane. He wept when His beloved Father forsook Him on the cross.

All the sorrows, disappointments, and failures which wring tears from your broken heart, He understands, for He endured them all and far more.

I know for some of you this Christmas is especially difficult, for it may be the first one you have faced since that dear one died, or since your marriage was torn apart, or since your life just seemed to cave in. You feel destitute, lonely, and forsaken. Like my poor mother so many years ago, you have endured what seems to be the straw that broke the camel's back and your heart. I cannot stand up and tell you things in this world will get better for you; they may or may not. I can't tell you the worst is over, or event that there will be a ten-dollar bill and a box of toys in the next day's mail. But what I can and do tell you is that our God has told us that when all the final effects of Christmas have taken place, there will never be a reason to cry again, except for sheer unending joy. For, "There will be no more death, nor sorrow, nor crying, nor pain, nor curse, for all these things will pass away. And His servants will serve Him, and they shall see His face, and there shall be no night there, for the Lord God gives them light, and they shall reign forever and ever."

Yes, it's okay to cry at Christmas if your heart is sad. Tears are God's gift for now. But He has better things in store for you in heaven where you'll never weep again or have any reason for tears. Many of you no doubt will be participating in a Christmas Eve communion service. The supper displayed before you will remind you of that night long ago when Jesus was eating the Passover with His disciples. The Word tells us He was deeply grieved and troubled at heart, saying, "One of you will betray me, and all of you will forsake me." A little later when alone in the Garden, he fell on His face and wept sorely with a breaking heart. But though weeping may endure for a night, joy comes in the morning, and so it did on that morning we call Easter, and so it shall on that morning we will call Glory. If you have tears to shed over the sorrows of your broken heart and shattered dreams, then let them flow freely with no shame. But never forget God will wipe away all tears from your eyes and heart.

Years after I had burned up the family Christmas, my mother told me that she had taken me to bed with her and both of us cried most of the night, but before she got up, she had hugged and kissed away my tears. I think that is exactly what God plans to do with you and me when the time comes, for He said, "Even as a mother comforts her child, so will I comfort you, and you will be comforted." So if you can't dry your tears tonight, it's okay. God will. That's what Christmas and Christmas Eve communion are all about. It's okay if your tears mingle with His when you drink the cup, for after His tears and yours, joy comes because of Christmas. Believe this. Go ahead and shed your tears on Christmas. Then wait in faith for Him to dry your tears; and He will wipe away all tears from your eyes forever and ever.

With sincere love and many prayers,

Gordon and Miriam Reed

Christmas: Believe It!

A Christmas Eve Communion Meditation

> In the sixth month the angel Gabriel was sent from God to a city of Galilee named Nazareth, 27 to a virgin betrothed to a man whose name was Joseph, of the house of David. And the virgin's name was Mary. 28 And he came to her and said, "Greetings, O favored one, the Lord is with you!" 29 But she was greatly troubled at the saying, and tried to discern what sort of greeting this might be. 30 And the angel said to her, "Do not be afraid, Mary, for you have found favor with God. 31 And behold, you will conceive in your womb and bear a son, and you shall call his name Jesus. 32 He will be great and will be called the Son of the Most High. And the Lord God will give to him the throne of his father David, 33 and he will reign over the house of Jacob forever, and of his kingdom there will be no end." 34 And Mary said to the angel, "How will this be, since I am a virgin?" 35 And the angel answered her, "The Holy Spirit will come upon you, and the power of the Most High will overshadow you; therefore the child to be born will be called holy—the Son of God. 36 And behold, your relative Elizabeth in her old age has also conceived a son, and this is the sixth month with her who was called barren. 37 For nothing will be impossible with God." 38 And Mary said, "Behold, I am the servant of the Lord; let it be to me according to your word." And the angel departed from her.
>
> *- Luke 1:26-38*

When the Holy Spirit awakens those who are dead in their trespasses and sins and quickens their minds to turn towards God, one of the first thoughts in response to this is the question Mary asked long ago. "How can these things be?" But the spirit and attitude in which this question is asked is totally changed. Before the work of grace begins, the question is often asked in stubborn resistance, rebellion, and maybe even ridicule. But then the Spirit moves, a longing begins to grow, there is a hunger and thirst for God, and the question is raised in a new spirit of eagerness and humility. "Are these things really true? How can these things be?" That was the attitude of young Mary when the angel Gabriel was sent from God to announce the coming birth of the Savior.

So many people missed Christmas, or almost missed it, and many still do right in the midst of this wonderful season. There were many reasons why people like the inn keeper, King Herod, the chief priests and rulers of the people, and the nation of Israel as a whole missed Christmas, but the one common thread that bound them together in the bundle of condemnation was unbelief.

But then for those who found Christmas — including Mary, the shepherds, the wise men, and Joseph and others — the one thing they had in common was that they believed what God said was true, and that belief led to saving faith, and true faith led to a level of commitment that still challenges us today. The same principles of unbelief and faith still mark the great divide between those who find and those who miss the true message of Christmas. But for each of these, faith came in a different way and required different responses.

I. First There was Mary

Picture the scene. Mary as a young girl in her teens, of royal blood but peasant circumstances, happily awaiting her marriage to good Joseph, the carpenter. Like all good Jews, she prayed every day for the Messiah to come, and for Israel to be free and great. Perhaps it was while praying this prayer that the angel Gabriel was sent from God to tell her that her prayers were answered, and far more. She would conceive and bear a son, and it would be He who would save His people from their sins. It would be He who would inherit the throne of David and reign over the house of Israel forever. And wonder of wonders, He would be the Son of God. In answer to her question, "How is this possible since I am unmarried and a virgin," the angel told her that the Holy Spirit would come upon her and by His power she would conceive and bear this child. All right, Mary, you've been praying for the Messiah to come, and now this is how God plans to bring it to pass. Here is what she had to believe:

1. She really talked with Gabriel.
2. She was going to be the mother of the Messiah.
3. She would conceive by the Holy Spirit.
4. Her son would reign over the house of Israel forever.
5. He is God in human nature.

Would she believe it? Here were the risks incurred:

1. Maybe she was out of her mind.
2. Joseph would break the betrothal.
3. She would be stoned to death.
4. If not stoned, she would live in utter disgrace the rest of her short and miserable life.

Believing what God reveals is really true always requires true faith and the commitment to risk everything this world values and respects. Her response might have been, "But Lord, don't you realize what this would mean?" But her response was, "Be it unto me according to your word." That, Beloved, is faith at its best, and commitment at its most sincere. God requires nothing less from each of us.

II. Then There was Joseph

If Mary had much to believe and all to risk, so did Joseph, her fiancé. Now let your mind picture Joseph. Mary, being the kind of person she was, went to Joseph, probably after her three-month visit with her cousin Elizabeth, and told him what was beginning to be obvious: she was pregnant. Of course, she related her encounter with the angel, but that took an awful lot of believing, and he could not. Not yet. But as he was grieving and planning how best to break the betrothal vows, God's angel came to him, too. The same angel that came to Mary? Probably. Now consider what Joseph had to believe:

1. Mary was telling the truth.
2. She was indeed pregnant, but still a virgin.
3. Her pregnancy was not of ordinary human conception, but of the Holy Spirit.
4. He was to take her as his wife and be the earthly foster-father of the Messiah.

Only by the same indwelling of the Holy Spirit that Mary had experienced in a different way could he ever believe these things. Just as you can never believe these same incredible truths until the Holy Spirit regenerates you and enables you to believe. The cost for Joseph?

1. Swallow your pride and male ego, Joseph. There is something far more important than this.
2. Become the kind of man you want this infant Jesus to be within your limitations, and guard Him and Mary with your life.

In short, it's commitment with no reservations. Joseph's believing response might well have been summed up in these words, "Be it unto her and me according to your word."

III. The Shepherds Had a Lot of Believing to Do, Too

When the time arrived, and God had arranged everything just right, Jesus was born in Bethlehem according to the ancient prophecies. You know the words and the familiar story: "And there were in the same country, shepherds abiding in the fields, keeping watch over their flocks by night…" Now it was their turn to see and hear angels. (By the way, there are few if any accounts in Scripture of anyone ever seeing an angel who wasn't frightened nearly to death. So much for our conception of what they look like.) When God's angel stood before them and the glory of heaven shone round about them, they, too, were afraid. Then the angel revealed the incredible. The Messiah they had long prayed for was born that very night in that little town so near at hand. Not only this, but He had come in lowly form and state, just like these lowly folk, and He had come to save them from their sins and make them sons of the Most High. Talk about believing! They were nobodies. These were simple, poor outcasts, despised and rejected by their own people. And God thinks they are important? So important that He sent angels from heaven to tell them of His grace and favor? And what did they have to believe?

1. The angels were real.
2. Their message was true.
3. They were important to God.
4. They could see for themselves if they would find the stable and manger.

One of the greatest tests of faith is always just at this point. God knows you. You are important to Him and loved so much that He gave His only begotten Son that if you would believe in Him, you should not perish but have everlasting life. Remember these words: "Unto you is born today, a Savior …" So, "today if you hear His voice, do not harden your heart." Go and find the manger, come and experience for yourself what countless millions have already discovered. God really did become a man one day. Of course, this required a great miracle — in fact, a series of them — but is that so strange? Would it not have been even more strange if the supernatural was not involved in all this? Does it take a lot of believing? Of course it does! Furthermore, when faith is sincere and real, it leads to the kind of commitment that is just as demanding as the faith of Mary, Joseph, and the shepherds. Would you expect less? Because people have believed this, oceans have been crossed, difficulties and dangers have been bravely faced and overcome, and crosses have been borne, death accepted as the inevitable result of believing what Mary and Joseph believed. But lives have been gloriously transformed and rescued, millions have heard and believed the Gospel and, praise God, Christmas has endured and will endure until the Lord shall come again.

Christmas? Believe it! Just remember what happened to people who believed the incredible, and don't forget what happened and happens to those who refused to believe.

Now here we are at this table, and the meaning of this requires faith — the same sort of faith Mary, Joseph, and the shepherds demonstrated of old. By this simple means of faith God has provided, we are united to Christ. We are recipients of the greatest gift ever given: salvation and eternal life forever in heaven with the Lord.

Christmas? Believe it! Receive it!

O Come, All Ye Faithful

Words: John Francis Wade (1711-1786), ca. 1743;
       tr. Frederick Oakeley (1802-1880) and others
Music: Present form of melody att. John Francis Wade (1711-1786), ca. 1743

Tune: *Adeste fideles*

5. Child, for us sinners
   poor and in the manger,
   we would embrace thee
   with and love and awe;
   who would not love thee,
   loving us so dearly? *Refrain*

6. Yea, Lord, we greet thee,
   born this happy morning;
   Jesus, to thee —
   be — glory given;
   Word of the Father,
   now in flesh appearing; *Refrain*

8. Lo! Star-led chieftains,
   magi, Christ adoring,
   offer Him frankincense
   and gold and myrrh;
   we to the Christ-child,
   bring our hearts oblations: *Refrain*

Hymn Notes

The origin of this hymn was a mystery for centuries. The text was variously ascribed to St. Bonaventure, the 13th century Italian scholar; Portuguese, German, and Spanish authors; and the Cistercian order of monks. Credit for the music was given to several 17th century English organists, a Portuguese musician, and George F. Handel. The shroud of mystery was torn away in 1946 when the Rev. Maurice Frost of Deddington, Oxford, discovered a manuscript of the hymn written in Latin. The next year, John Stéphan, a Benedictine monk, published a dissertation titled *The Adeste Fideles: A Study On Its Origin and Development* (Devon, 1947), in which he concluded that hymn and tune were both written by an Englishman named John Francis Wade. That conclusion is generally accepted by scholars today. Wade wrote the text in Latin in four stanzas. The earliest manuscript bearing his signature is dated ca. 1743. By the early 19th century, four additional stanzas had been added by other writers.

By 1731, Wade had moved to France, presumably to escape religious persecution in England against Roman Catholics. He made a living by hand copying plainchant at the Dominican college in Bornhem, Flanders; teaching music at an English college in Douai, France; and copying and selling chant music for use in the chapels of wealthy families. These manuscripts were published as *Cantus Diversi pro Dominicis et Festis per annum* (1751).

The English translation of *O come, all ye faithful* in common usage today is largely the work of Englishman Frederick Oakeley, who translated the text for use at the Margaret Street Chapel in London in 1841. Educated at Christ Church, Oxford, Oakeley was ordained in the Church of England in 1826. He served several pastorates before becoming involved in the era's Oxford Movement, a factor that prompted him to leave the Anglican Church and seek ordination in the Roman Catholic Church in 1845. Following his reordination, Oakeley's work included serving among the poor in the Westminster area of London.

-TW

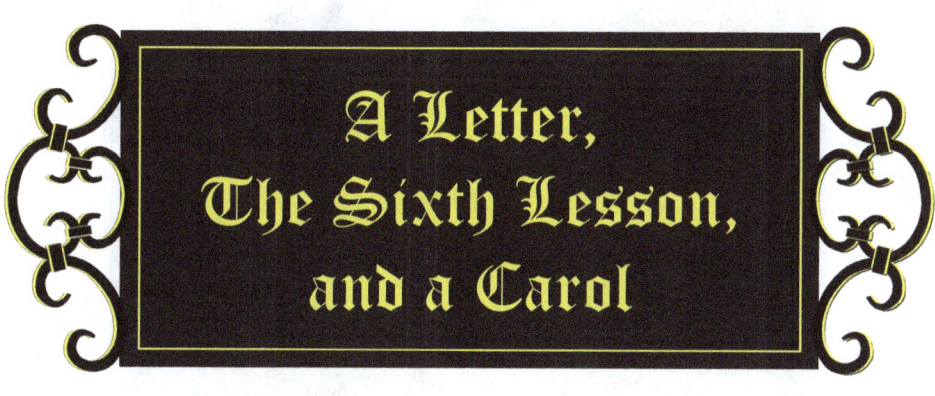

Panel with Angel Appearing to Zacharias, 15th century

Domingo Ram (1464-1507), Spain

Tempera on wood, gold ground

Metropolitan Museum of Art Open Access Collection

Zacharias, father of John the Baptist, appears here in elaborate dress. The pendant bells and pomegranates adorning his robe denote his function as the high priest. He is depicted fulfilling his annual and privileged duty to enter the Holy of Holies of the temple in Jerusalem to make sacrifice on behalf of the people. The rope tied around his ankle is held by another priest, whose job it would be to pull Zacharias out if he were to die while in the Holy of Holies, as no one else was permitted to enter the sacred space. According to Luke 1:5-25, it was while Zacharias was in the act of fulfilling this duty that an angel appeared and announced that Zacharias and his wife, Elizabeth - both advanced in years - would be the parents of John the Baptist.

Christmas Angels

Dearly Beloved,

God grant you a joyful and merry Christmas time. This year, I want to talk about God's holy and blessed Christmas angels. I have always loved these stories from God's Word about the angels of Christmas. Even as a very small child, I loved to hear about the angels God sent down from heaven to prepare the world for the coming of the Christ Child. There is something about angels, and especially the Christmas angels, that appeals to our sense of need for that which we cannot see but know is real.

The role of the angels of Christmas begins with the appearance of the angel to the elderly priest Zacharias as he was preparing to burn incense in the temple at Jerusalem as a part of the ceremonies of worship. This was probably the last time this good man would participate in the temple worship before being retired from active service. When the heavenly visitor spoke to Zacharias, he told him that he and his wife Elizabeth would have a son, even in their old age, who would be the forerunner of the coming Messiah. This angel was Gabriel, who was sent by God to tell Zacharias the honor which God had bestowed on him and his wife.

This same angel Gabriel was sent to the young Virgin Mary to bring the joyful news that by the power of God's Holy Spirit she would conceive a son in her womb who would be the promised Messiah God's people had waited for, for many generations. When Joseph, her betrothed husband, discovered that Mary was expecting a child, he was brokenhearted until the angel of God appeared to him in a dream, reassuring him the child Mary carried in her womb was the Son of God! Furthermore, Joseph was instructed to call His name 'Jesus' for He would save God's people from their sins.

Later, Joseph and Mary were ordered to go to Bethlehem to be enrolled in the census decreed by Caesar Augustus. There in a lowly cattle stall, Jesus was born. Now many angels were sent by God to the lowliest of the low, a group of shepherds who lived outside of Bethlehem and were in the fields keeping watch over their flocks by night. These angels brought the long awaited and joyful news that the Savior had at last been born in a stable in Bethlehem. Believing the angels, they made their way to the place where Jesus was born to see for themselves that God really had sent them a Savior.

Just as the angels had announced to these shepherds this incredible news that Jesus was born, these lowly shepherds went everywhere spreading the good tidings of great joy. So this Christmas season we, too, may help spread the news that God sent down His Son Jesus to be our Savior. No, we are not likely to hear angels announcing the birth of our Savior to the people of this world ... but we can! Let's just do it.

Merry love-filled Christmas, dearly beloved.

Gordon   Miriam

The Reeds, Miriam and Gordon

We Hear the Christmas Angels, Their Great Glad Tidings Tell
Part 1: The Angel of Anticipation

In the days of Herod, king of Judea, there was a priest named Zacharias, of the division of Abijah. And he had a wife from the daughters of Aaron, and her name was Elizabeth. ⁶And they were both righteous before God, walking blamelessly in all the commandments and statutes of the Lord. ⁷But they had no child, because Elizabeth was barren, and both were advanced in years. ⁸Now while he was serving as priest before God when his division was on duty, ⁹according to the custom of the priesthood, he was chosen by lot to enter the temple of the Lord and burn incense. ¹⁰And the whole multitude of the people were praying outside at the hour of incense. ¹¹And there appeared to him an angel of the Lord standing on the right side of the altar of incense. ¹²And Zacharias was troubled when he saw him, and fear fell upon him. ¹³But the angel said to him, "Do not be afraid, Zacharias, for your prayer has been heard, and your wife Elizabeth will bear you a son, and you shall call his name John. ¹⁴And you will have joy and gladness, and many will rejoice at his birth, ¹⁵for he will be great before the Lord. And he must not drink wine or strong drink, and he will be filled with the Holy Spirit, even from his mother's womb. ¹⁶And he will turn many of the children of Israel to the Lord their God, ¹⁷and he will go before him in the spirit and power of Elijah, to turn the hearts of the fathers to the children, and the disobedient to the wisdom of the just, to make ready for the Lord a people prepared." ¹⁸And Zacharias said to the angel, "How shall I know this? For I am an old man, and my wife is advanced in years." ¹⁹And the angel answered him, "I am Gabriel. I stand in the presence of God, and I was sent to speak to you and to bring you this good news. ²⁰And behold, you will be silent and unable to speak until the day that these things take place, because you did not believe my words, which will be fulfilled in their time." ²¹And the people were waiting for Zacharias, and they were wondering at his delay in the temple. ²²And when he came out, he was unable to speak to them, and they realized that he had seen a vision in the temple. And he kept making signs to them and remained mute. ²³And when his time of service was ended, he went to his home. ²⁴After these days his wife Elizabeth conceived, and for five months she kept herself hidden, saying, ²⁵"Thus the Lord has done for me in the days when he looked on me, to take away my reproach among people."

- Luke 1:5-25

In every story in the New Testament concerning the birth of Christ, angels appear and have a prominent role in this incredible unfolding story of salvation. Many of the hymns we still sing either quote the words of angels or tell of their part in the story of Christ's birth. Yet, angels are so remote from our own experiences and understanding that we seldom give a thought to their existence or to their importance, if any. Still, it can't be denied that everywhere you turn in the Christmas story, angels are there — speaking, singing, proclaiming the good news, rebuking the unbelieving, and bringing renewed hope to those who had lost all hope.

But where are the angels today? Why don't we still see them and hear messages from them, for after all, the word 'angel' simply means 'messenger'? There is a very good reason why few, if any, of us ever have any real encounters with angels. The book of Hebrews tells us that the primary role of angels was to deliver God's revelation in days now past. But since the completion of the New Testament, there is no longer a need for or any evidence of any new revelation. God's word is complete.

So, it seems that angels have slipped back into obscurity for the most part. We are only told that they are ministering spirits to believers. Beyond that, we know little, if anything, about their present ministry. But when Christ returns, once again angels will have a very prominent place. If you ever see one, be nice to it (him? her?) because angels will be "gathering the elect from the four winds of the earth," and will be appointed by God to separate true believers from false pretenders. They will be God's agents of both mercy and judgment.

The first "Christmas angel" we meet in the story of Christ's birth is the angel who announced the birth of John the Baptist, and that's where the story of Christmas begins.

I. The Childless Couple Who Met the First Angel

It was a dark and hopeless time in the life of God's people. They had frittered away their hard-earned freedom, bought by the blood of their forebears. Their ruler was a man who had sold his soul to gain the throne. He was a grasping, greedy, and bloody tyrant whose only ambition was his own power and control. All longed for the promised Messiah. Few believed He would come, and even fewer understood what His coming would really mean.

In this situation of despair, the spotlight of Scripture falls upon two old people: a priest named Zacharias and his wife, Elizabeth, who was the daughter of a priest. Significantly, the name 'Zacharias' means "the Lord remembers His covenant," and the name Elizabeth means, "my God is faithful." Little did they know how true their names would be. They were childless — the ultimate tragedy for a Jewish couple — and they were now well beyond childbearing years. However, their deep disappointment did not cause them to be bitter or indifferent towards God. They went about their lives, "righteous in the sight of God, walking blamelessly in all the commandments and requirements of the Lord." That's how life is in this fallen world. It is filled with disappointments, frustrated ambitions, and empty dreams. But believers press on.

For Zacharias, the best he could hope for in his service as a priest was that one day he might be allowed to offer the incense offering when the people gathered for worship. That doesn't sound like much, but a priest would make this offering only once in his entire life, and not all had that honor. So, as thousands gathered in the temple court to worship and pray, Zacharias entered the Holy Place, just outside the Holiest of Holies, to burn the incense before the Lord. When the signal was given, the people saw the cloud of incense rising from the altar and fell down on their faces. At this time, there was total silence for several minutes while they prayed and waited for the priest to come out before them and pronounce the benediction of assurance that their prayers were heard, their sins forgiven.

II. The Message of Hope

It was during this time of sacred waiting that suddenly an angel came to Zacharias, standing just beside the altar where the incense was rising towards heaven. He calmed the natural fright of this good man and went on to say, "Your petition has been heard, and you and Elizabeth will have a son. You will have joy and gladness, and many will rejoice at his birth." This startling announcement was followed by an even greater revelation. This son was to be the promised messenger who would prepare the way for the Messiah. He would be like Elijah of old, a mighty prophet. He would lead the nation in its greatest revival, and many people would turn back to the Lord because of this coming son.

At last, at long last, there is hope. God has remembered His covenant and God is faithful. To a man whose brightest and best moment was the one time in His life when he was allowed to offer the incense offering and to assure the people of sins forgiven, there came a far greater moment of glory and wonder. The hopes and fears of all the years had suddenly come to his doorstep and into his heart.

III. The Faltering Faith and Coming Sign

Sometimes, God asks us to believe the most impossible things! Disobedience to His commands brings misery and death? Nonsense! Why, anyone could see that the fruit in the midst of the garden was good to eat, a delight to the eyes, and so obviously the way to wisdom and happiness.

"Through your son, Isaac, you will have a multitude of descendants. Now take him to Moriah and offer him for a burnt offering." Impossible!

The desert behind you, the Red Sea before you, and Pharoah's cavalry charging, "Now speak to the people and march forward, and watch the waters open for a path."

"Behold, a virgin shall conceive and bear a Son and you will call Him Emmanuel, God with us."

Try this one: "Believe on the Lord Jesus Christ, and you will be saved."

Now to this good, old priest and his elderly wife, God said, "Don't be afraid. God has heard your prayers and you will have a son, and you will name him John, which means 'the gracious gift of God'." Would you believe if you were in his shoes?

So, Zacharias stumbled. He had prayed all his life for a son. He had prayed all his life for the Messiah to come. Now God said, "Your prayers have been answered." Zacharias said, "Show me a sign of proof. After all, we're just two old people." The angel answered, "But I am Gabriel who stands in the presence of God." In effect, he was saying, "You are not just doubting me, you are doubting the word of God." Gabriel was the special messenger of God. He was closer to God than any other being and he always brings good news every time he appears in Scripture. When God reveals the gospel of grace through His Son, failure to respond and accept that good news is to deny God and doubt His word.

"So, Zaccharias, you doubt the word of God? Here then is your sign. You will be stricken dumb and unable to speak until God's promise comes true." Be careful how you even think in the depths of your secret heart, "God prove yourself to me." He may just do that in a way you don't want Him to. He could fry you with a bolt of lightning!

When Zaccharias finally came out to bring the people the assurance of God's forgiveness and that their prayers had been answered, this moment for which he had lived and looked forward to all his life passed him by. He was unable to say those blessed words of the Aaronic benediction, or any word at all.

Unbelief and doubt have a heavy price, but God who is merciful had the last word. Gabriel's promise came true. Zacharias and Elizabeth had their son. Their hearts had been cleansed of sinful doubts, and when John (remember, his name means 'God's gracious gift') was born, Zacharias spoke his first words in nine months, and they were simply these: "His name is John." In saying those words, he revealed his repentance and faith.

Thirty years later, the greatest religious awakening since the days of Elijah broke out in Israel. Many hearts were turned to God. Many lives were changed. One day, John was able to point to a young man named Jesus and say, "Behold the Lamb of God who takes away the sin of the world."

Soon, his short life was over, but John's mission had been accomplished. God has a purpose in the life of each believer. Sometimes, we do not fully understand what that purpose is and why some are taken seemingly before their time. But the God who will wipe away all of our earthly tears will one day display His glorious purposes, and our hearts will be mended, completely and permanently.

Zacharias' prayer was answered. The imperfect sacrifice and prayer he had offered in the earthly temple was replaced by our great High Priest Jesus, who offered the perfect prayer and sacrifice, thus opening the door of heaven to you and me.

Oh, yes, we still "hear the Christmas angels, their great glad tidings tell." So, we pray, "O holy Child of Bethlehem! Descend to us, we pray; cast out our sins and enter in, be born in us today! We hear the Christmas angels, the great glad tidings tell; O come to us, abide with us, our Lord Emmanuel."

May we learn by faith the lesson Zacharias learned the hard way and believe the promises of God; the promises of sin forgiven through the perfect sacrifice of our Lord Jesus, and the best promise of all: heaven is ours because Jesus left heaven and came to earth one day, not so very long ago. And He's coming again, but that's another part of the story.

O Little Town of Bethlehem

4. Where children pure and happy
   Pray to the blessed Child,
   Where misery cries out to thee
   Son of the mother mild;
   Where charity stands watching
   And faith holds wide the door,
   The dark night wakes, the glory breaks,
   And Christmas comes once more.

5. O holy Child of Bethlehem,
   Descend to us, we pray;
   Cast out our sin and enter in;
   Be born in us today.
   We hear the Christmas angels
   The great glad tidings tell;
   O come to us, abide with us,
   Our Lord Emmanuel.

Words: Phillips Brooks (1835-1893), 1868
Music: Lewis Henry Redner (1831-1908), 1868

Tune: *St. Louis*

Hymn Notes

In 1865, the year that the Civil War ended, Phillips Brooks spent a year traveling abroad and was in Bethlehem at Christmastime. He rode on horseback through the fields around Bethlehem and attended the Church of the Nativity on Christmas Eve. The trip likely inspired this carol, but it was not completed until 1868. Following is a passage from a letter that Brooks wrote home while in Bethlehem.

> After an early dinner, we took our horses and rode to Bethlehem. It was only about two hours when we came to the town, situated on an eastern ridge of a range of hills, surrounded by its terraced gardens. It is a good-looking town, better built than any other we have seen in Palestine. . . . Before dark, we rode out of town to the field where they say the shepherds saw the star. It is a fenced piece of ground with a cave in it (all the Holy Places are caves here), in which, strangely enough, they put the shepherds. The story is absurd, but somewhere in those fields we rode through the shepherds must have been. . . . As we passed, the shepherds were still "keeping watch over their flocks" or "leading them home to fold."   - *Louis F. Benson, "Studies Of Familiar Hymns"*

At the time the carol was completed, Brooks was rector of Holy Trinity Episcopal Church in Philadelphia. That year, he commissioned a tune for his text from his church organist, Lewis H. Redner, so that it could be sung at the Sunday school Christmas service on December 27, 1868. In addition to serving as organist at Holy Trinity, Redner (a wealthy real estate broker by profession) was superintendent of the church's mission and a Sunday school teacher. Of Brooks' request for a tune to accompany his carol, Redner wrote in part:

> As Christmas of 1868 approached, Mr. Brooks told me that he had written a simple little carol for the Christmas Sunday-school service, and he asked me to write the tune to it. The simple music was written in great haste and under great pressure. We were to practice it on the following Sunday. Mr. Brooks came to me on Friday, and said, "Redner, have you ground out that music yet to *O Little Town of Bethlehem*?" I replied, "No," but that he should have it by Sunday. On the Saturday night previous my brain was all confused about the tune. I thought more about my Sunday-school lesson than I did about the music. But I was roused from sleep late in the night hearing an angel-strain whispering in my ear, and seizing a piece of music paper I jotted down the treble of the tune as we now have it, and on Sunday morning before going to church I filled in the harmony. Neither Mr. Brooks nor I ever thought the carol or the music to it would live beyond that Christmas of 1868 … Rev. Dr. Huntington, rector of All Saints' Church, Worcester, Mass., asked permission to print it in his Sunday-school hymn and tune book, called *The Church Porch*, and it was he who christened the music 'Saint Louis'.   - *Louis F. Benson, "Studies Of Familiar Hymns"*

The poignancy of this carol contrasts dramatically with the many Christmas carols that emphasize the glory of God as seen in the throng of heralding angels. British hymnologist J.R. Watson sums it up thusly: "Not only does the hymn beautifully describe the little town asleep in the December night; it also gracefully modulates from a description of Christmas into an examination of the meaning of Christmas: first in its encouragement of charity and faith, and then into the coming of Christ into the human heart."   - *TW*

The Holy Family, ca. 1520

Gerard David (ca. 1460-1523), Netherlands

Oil on panel

The Metropolitan Museum of Art Open Access Collection

Gerard David worked primarily for churches, monasteries, convents, and magistrates. His work is known for a quality of intimacy, subdued coloring, and a rendering of faces uncharacteristic of the era: almond-shaped eyes, thick eyelids, straight mouths, pronounced chins, and high foreheads. He is also known for his realistic representation of everyday objects, such as the apples and bowl in this painting, and is regarded as something of a trailblazer in terms of his treatment of landscapes.

The rotten apples that Joseph holds in this painting are meant to recall the fall of Adam and thus symbolize the Christ Child's destiny.

We Hear the Christmas Angels, Their Great Glad Tidings Tell
Part 2: Good News: Gabriel and Mary

A CHRISTMAS EVE COMMUNION MEDITATION

In the sixth month the angel Gabriel was sent from God to a city of Galilee named Nazareth, 27 to a virgin betrothed to a man whose name was Joseph, of the house of David. And the virgin's name was Mary. 28 And he came to her and said, "Greetings, O favored one, the Lord is with you!" 29 But she was greatly troubled at the saying, and tried to discern what sort of greeting this might be. 30 And the angel said to her, "Do not be afraid, Mary, for you have found favor with God. 31 And behold, you will conceive in your womb and bear a son, and you shall call his name Jesus. 32 He will be great and will be called the Son of the Most High. And the Lord God will give to him the throne of his father David, 33 and he will reign over the house of Jacob forever, and of his kingdom there will be no end." 34 And Mary said to the angel, "How will this be, since I am a virgin?" 35 And the angel answered her, "The Holy Spirit will come upon you, and the power of the Most High will overshadow you; therefore the child to be born will be called holy—the Son of God. 36 And behold, your relative Elizabeth in her old age has also conceived a son, and this is the sixth month with her who was called barren. 37 For nothing will be impossible with God." 38 And Mary said, "Behold, I am the servant of the Lord; let it be to me according to your word." And the angel departed from her.

- Luke 1:26-38

☙

And Mary said, "My soul magnifies the Lord, 47 and my spirit rejoices in God my Savior, 48 for he has looked on the humble estate of his servant. For behold, from now on all generations will call me blessed; 49 for he who is mighty has done great things for me, and holy is his name. 50 And his mercy is for those who fear him from generation to generation. 51 He has shown strength with his arm; he has scattered the proud in the thoughts of their hearts; 52 he has brought down the mighty from their thrones and exalted those of humble estate; 53 he has filled the hungry with good things, and the rich he has sent away empty. 54 He has helped his servant Israel, in remembrance of his mercy, 55 as he spoke to our fathers, to Abraham and to his offspring forever." 56 And Mary remained with her about three months and returned to her home.

- Luke 1:46-56

Who was Mary? From all outward appearance, just a small town peasant girl about to be married to a nice, steady carpenter who lived in the same town. Yet, we learn from Luke that there was far more to Mary than appeared on the surface. Was she a descendant from David as was her husband-to-be, Joseph? If so, how would we know? Many have noted the slight variations in Matthew's and Luke's genealogical lists and see this as evidence that Luke was really giving us Mary's lineage, but we really don't know if that's the case.

We have far more conclusive evidence that Mary was indeed an heir of kings from what Gabriel said about the child she would bear. Listen to this: "The Lord God will give Him the throne of His father, David, and He will reign over the house of Israel forever." Then, Gabriel revealed to Mary that her conception would not be by ordinary human generation, but by the power of the Holy Spirit. So, since He had no earthly father, and since David was called his ancestor, it would seem a logical conclusion that Mary, like Joseph, was also a descendant of David.

There is another side to Mary's lineage that is equally impressive. Gabriel said that her cousin Elizabeth was already six months pregnant. Remember, Elizabeth was the daughter of a priest, a descendant of the first high priest, Aaron. So, Mary was not only descended from the great king David; she was also descended from the high priest as well. Not a bad lineage for a little nobody country girl!

I. Gabriel is Sent to Mary

I love the way Martin Luther used his vivid imagination to describe this unlikely encounter between the highest of angels and the lowest of lowly. He reminds us that the Jews were an oppressed and downtrodden people at this time, and that Mary was one of the lowliest, being a small town girl of peasant parents. Luther went on to say, "Quite possibly, she was doing the housework when the angel Gabriel came to her." That's a guess on Luther's part, but as good a guess as any. What a contrast! This is Gabriel who stands in the presence of God, and this is Mary, young peasant girl in a small and insignificant town.

The greeting of Gabriel was not, "Hail Mary, full of grace" as the Latin translates this passage, but rather, "Rejoice, highly favored one, the Lord is with you; blessed are you among women." This certainly means that Mary was the object of grace, not the source of grace as some would have it. Nevertheless, the honor was great to be visited by the highest angel in heaven and to be told that God's special grace rested upon her.

Mary's reaction was the same as yours would have been. She was frightened and mystified. Who was she to receive a special revelation from God? Who was she to be told that God's grace rested upon her in a wonderful way? But then, who am I that God's saving grace should reach such a sinner as I? Why would God make any of us the object of His special love and mercy? Mary's fear did not prevent her from wanting to know the meaning of God's word to her, and Gabriel knew it.

II. The Amazing Message of Gabriel to Mary

First, Gabriel quieted Mary's fears, and then comforted her with these words: "Fear not Mary, for you have found favor with God ..." How amazingly similar is this whole situation and these words to what had happened long before to a man named Noah. In the midst of the wicked and hopeless situation we read, "Noah found grace in the eyes of the Lord," and through his God-given faith, salvation came. Now here is little Mary in a time of hopelessness and empty despair being told, "You have found grace in the sight of the Lord, and through you the Savior will come."

Then, Gabriel revealed to her in these words the most incredible news of all time: "And behold, you will conceive in your womb, and bring forth a son, and shall call His name Jesus. He will be great, and will be called the Son of the Highest; and the Lord God will give Him the throne of His father, David. And He will reign over the house of Jacob forever, and of His kingdom there will be no end."

Mary's response was natural. She was a young maiden but she knew the basic facts of reproduction, and she also knew and said that she was pure and chaste. How was it possible then for her to have a baby, and even more for that baby to be both King and Savior? When we are presented with seemingly impossible things such as the virgin birth ... but even more, God becoming man, and even more than that, the miracle of the new birth within our own hearts ... it is so easy to dismiss it all as nonsense, and so difficult to believe these things. But God presents Himself to us in just this way and gives to us exceedingly great and precious promises, and calls on us to believe and act upon His word. There are two ways to ask the question, "How can these things be?" We may ask it with scornful unbelief, or, when we are perplexed with things beyond our understanding as Mary was, we may ask in her humble spirit. God answers and assures those who ask in that humble spirit.

III. The Angel's Assurance and Mary's Submission

So, Mary's honest yet humble question deserved and received God's answer. This is one of the first New Testament assertions of the Trinity. Listen to these words: "The Holy Spirit will come upon you, and the power of the Most High will overshadow you; and for that reason, the holy offspring will be called the Son of God." Just as we find the Trinity at work in the creation of the world in Genesis 1, so now at the beginning of the Gospel we hear once more of God's triune nature. "In the beginning, God created the heavens and the earth ... and the Spirit of God brooded upon the face of the waters ... and God said, let there be light and there was light."

Now, Mary will be the focus and object of God's new creative power. Bernard of Clairvaux in the twelfth century said:

"There are three miracles here:
1. that God and man should be joined in this child;
2. that Mary, though a virgin, should have this baby;
3. that Mary should have such faith as to believe this mystery would be accomplished in her.

The last is not the least of these three."

Luther added, "The virgin birth is a mere trifle for God; that God should become man is a greater miracle; but most amazing of all was that this little maiden would believe that she had been chosen to be the mother of God's Son."

Gabriel had a sign from God to encourage Mary to believe. "Your relative Elizabeth has also conceived a son in her old age, and she who was barren is even now in her sixth month. For nothing will be impossible with God."

Now comes Mary's incredible response of believing trust: "Be it unto me according to your word." Just that; no more nor less. She knew (or thought she knew) she would certainly lose Joseph. She knew she would probably face death or disgrace or both, but God called and she heard. God commanded and she obeyed. God offered and she accepted.

IV. Mary's Joy

It was not lack of faith, but need for assurance that caused Mary to make a hasty journey to the hill country of Judea to see her cousin Elizabeth. What a joyful reunion they had. You know the story of how Elizabeth greeted Mary and the baby she now carried, and how her own prenatal babe leaped for joy within her womb. They could only have known by revelation from God that Mary was now carrying the promised Messiah, and their faith reached out to Mary and gave her that assurance and confirmation she so needed.

Isn't that how God still works faith and makes it grow? Believer encourages believer. Your faith strengthens and confirms mine, and my faith helps you to believe even more. Elizabeth's joy was contagious and Mary broke out in joyful praise and glad worship. Freely paraphrasing Hannah's song when Samuel was conceived, she glorified God for remembering His gracious covenant and rescuing His downtrodden people. Joy, like faith, is still contagious, and our joy is like a warming fire to the coldhearted and cast down.

Can you sing Mary's song? Can you join her joy? O yes, if only you believe God's word, accept His Son as your Savior, and like Mary offer yourself to Him this Christmas and say to Him come what may, even through your pain, disappointment, and grief, "Be it unto me according to Your word." That is the very essence of faith, and blessed be the person who will answer back to God, even through pain and tears, these same believing, trusting words.

As we come once more to the Lord's Table this Christmas Eve, let us make sure that we understand the cost of true discipleship. Let us be prepared to respond to the word of God as Mary responded. Come what may under God's wise and loving hand of providence, may we answer back to Him, "Be it unto me according to Your word." Thus, we affirm our unqualified response to our Lord when He said, "If anyone will come after Me, let him deny himself and take up his cross and follow Me." The bread broken, the cup given are symbols of the sacrifice made for our salvation. Our reception of the elements with all their powerful meaning is our sincere and heartfelt rededication to walking the cross path our Master bids us trod.

Gabriel's Message

Words: Basque carol; paraphrased Sabine Baring-Gould (1834-1924)
Music: Basque carol; arr. Edgar Pettman (1886-1943)

Tune: *Gabriel's Message*

4. Then gentle Mary meekly bowed her head,
   "To me be as it pleaseth God," she said,
   "my soul shall laud and magnify his holy Name."
   Most highly favored lady, Gloria!

5. Of her, Emmanuel, the Christ, was born
   In Bethlehem, all on a Christmas morn,
   And Christian folk throughout the world
       will ever say—
   "Most highly favored lady," Gloria!

<u>Hymn Notes</u>

This lilting, almost dance-like carol relates the story of the Annunciation as recorded in Luke 1:26-55. It has been in the repertoire of Christmas music for more than 700 years. While the tune of this hymn is without question based on a traditional Basque carol, the origin of the text is slightly muddy. Some hymn historians believe it to be of Basque origin, while others cite as its source one of the several 13th century Latin hymns titled *Angelus ad Virginem (The angel to the maiden)*. Whether it is rooted in the Latin hymn or in a native Basque folk song, the carol found its way to the northern region of Spain and spread worldwide from there. It came into English usage with Sabine Baring-Gould's translation and paraphrase. During his childhood, Baring-Gould spent a winter in the Basque region, an excursion that planted the seed for his later interest in the music of the region. It is Baring-Gould who was responsible for the beautiful phrase 'wings as drifted snow' that occurs in the first stanza.

The Rev. Sabine Baring-Gould is the author of more than 100 books, but is perhaps best known for his hymns *Onward, Christian soldiers* and *Now the day is over*. He was married to a mill-girl half his age and the father of 15 children. As an Anglican priest, he served in a small Devonshire village while pursuing a variety of writing endeavors. He was considered one of the top novelists of his time, but also wrote about matters in such arenas as travel, history, and religion. Together with the books noted above, his literary output numbers over 1,200 publications. In his spare time, he dabbled in architecture and archaeology.

The Basque tune upon which *Gabriel's Message* is based, *Birjina gaztettobat zegoen*, was collected by French composer and musicologist Charles Bordes in a tour of the Basque country of northern Spain and published in his 1895 series *Archives de la tradition basque*, a collection of Basque folk tunes. Like Sabing-Gould, Bordes lived life to its fullest. He began his training as a student of the organist/composer César Franck. In 1890, he became chapelmaster of St. Gervais in Paris, but worked far beyond the perimeters of his job description to make the church a center for the study of the vocal music of the mid-Renaissance. In 1894, Bordes teamed with the renowned organist/composer Alexandre Guilmant to found the Paris Schola Cantorum, a society that became a school for the study of church music, and later started a branch of the school in Montpellier. He published two newsletters that provided pertinent information to music organizations and schools. As a composer, Bordes achieved particular success with his songs. He also composed piano music, sacred and secular choral works, a suite for flute and string quartet in the style of Basque music, and an orchestral work.

This carol's harmonization as given in most modern hymnals was arranged by Edgar Pettman and published in his collection, *Modern Christmas Carols* (1922). After completing his studies at the Royal Academy of Music in London, Pettman served as organist at a number of churches throughout England until 1915, after which he became a music editor. Pettman produced over a dozen hymn and carol collections, and took a special interest in working toward the revival of the European folk-carol.

-TW

Flight Into Egypt, 1923

Henry Ossawa Tanner (1859-1937), United States

Oil on canvas

The Metropolitan Museum of Art Open Access Collection

"Flight into Egypt" depicts the story of the Holy Family fleeing Herod's soldiers, who were sent to slay all little boys age two and under (Matthew 2:12-14). An angel appeared to Joseph in a dream to warn him of Herod's plot and instruct him to take his family to safety in Egypt. This is said to be Tanner's favorite Bible story; he created at least fifteen works on the theme. Tanner's personal experience of racism, which spurred him to move from the United States to Paris, may have caused him to feel particular empathy for the persecution that the Holy Family endured.

We Hear the Christmas Angels, Their Great Glad Tidings Tell
Part 3: Joseph the Dreamer

Now the birth of Jesus Christ took place in this way. When his mother Mary had been betrothed to Joseph, before they came together she was found to be with child from the Holy Spirit. [9] And her husband Joseph, being a just man and unwilling to put her to shame, resolved to divorce her quietly. [20] But as he considered these things, behold, an angel of the Lord appeared to him in a dream, saying, "Joseph, son of David, do not fear to take Mary as your wife, for that which is conceived in her is from the Holy Spirit. [21] She will bear a son, and you shall call his name Jesus, for he will save his people from their sins." [22] All this took place to fulfill what the Lord had spoken by the prophet: [23] "Behold, the virgin shall conceive and bear a son, and they shall call his name Immanuel" (which means, God with us). [24] When Joseph woke from sleep, he did as the angel of the Lord commanded him: he took his wife, [25] but knew her not until she had given birth to a son. And he called his name Jesus.

- Matthew 1:18-25

☙☞

Now when they had departed, behold, an angel of the Lord appeared to Joseph in a dream and said, "Rise, take the child and his mother, and flee to Egypt, and remain there until I tell you, for Herod is about to search for the child, to destroy him." [14] And he rose and took the child and his mother by night and departed to Egypt [15] and remained there until the death of Herod. This was to fulfill what the Lord had spoken by the prophet, "Out of Egypt I called my son." [16] Then Herod, when he saw that he had been tricked by the wise men, became furious, and he sent and killed all the male children in Bethlehem and in all that region who were two years old or under, according to the time that he had ascertained from the wise men. [17] Then was fulfilled what was spoken by the prophet Jeremiah: [18] "A voice was heard in Ramah, weeping and loud lamentation, Rachel weeping for her children; she refused to be comforted, because they are no more." [19] But when Herod died, behold, an angel of the Lord appeared in a dream to Joseph in Egypt, [20] saying, "Rise, take the child and his mother and go to the land of Israel, for those who sought the child's life are dead." [21] And he rose and took the child and his mother and went to the land of Israel. [22] But when he heard that Archelaus was reigning over Judea in place of his father Herod, he was afraid to go there, and being warned in a dream he withdrew to the district of Galilee. [23] And he went and lived in a city called Nazareth, so that what was spoken by the prophets might be fulfilled, that he would be called a Nazarene.

- Matthew 2:13-23

One of the most fascinating persons in the Old Testament is Joseph, the great grandson of Abraham, about whom we know so much. One of the most fascinating persons in the New Testament is Joseph, the husband of the Virgin Mary, about whom we know next to nothing. Yet, it is amazing how much they had in common. Both of their lives were greatly affected by dreams and both of them had sojourns in Egypt.

Remember the story of Joseph as told in the book of Genesis? He was the eleventh son of Jacob and the first by his beloved Rachel. His big brothers mocked him, calling him "that dreamer." Joseph was a dreamer. In fact, his dreams, and later the dreams of others, would shape and mold his life.

It all started when, as a young boy, he dreamed that he and his brothers were binding sheaves in the field, and suddenly his sheaf stood up and all the other sheaves of his brothers bowed down to it. When he told the dream to his brothers, they hated him even more than before. Then, he dreamed again and saw the sun and moon and eleven stars bowing down to him, indicating that one day even his parents would bow before him. You know the rest of that story; how his brothers plotted against him to kill him, but instead sold him into slavery into Egypt. There he rose quickly to a position of great power in an important household. But when he refused the advances of his master's wife, he was thrown into prison and was left there for years.

But, again, dreams began to offer hope. This time, it was not his dream but that of the chief butler, who had been thrown into prison for a suspected plot against Pharaoh. Joseph correctly interpreted the dream that the butler would be spared, and was promised help in being released from prison — which was promptly forgotten.

Still again, a dream affected him greatly. Mighty Pharaoh had a disturbing dream which none of his minions could interpret. Finally, the butler remembered his promise to Joseph and told Pharoah of the remarkable young man in prison who could interpret dreams. From there, Joseph went on to greatness and all his earlier dreams came true, as his whole family came and bowed before him.

Now let me tell you about another Joseph whose life was shaped and directed by dreams which always came just in the nick of time for him and his family. In each of these life changing and life saving dreams, Joseph saw and heard an angel with messages from God.

I. Joseph's First Encounter with An Angel

It all began just after Joseph received the shattering news that his beloved fiancée, Mary, was pregnant, and not by him. His options were few. He could either accuse her openly before the Sanhedrin and have her stoned to death, or he could privately break the betrothal and simply end the relationship without accusation. This he was planning to do, but at the same time his heart was broken, his dreams of happiness destroyed, and his hope for an heir gone. But note well that Joseph was not seeking personal revenge on Mary for embarrassing him before the world. Already, his qualifications for being the foster father of the Messiah began to manifest themselves. It was while he was thinking, planning, weeping over these things that he fell at last into an uneasy sleep.

In his God-sent sleep, a dream began to develop that was more than a dream. God's holy angel stood by his side to bring comfort and a message of great hope that dried his eyes, eased his heart, and opened his mind to a most wondrous truth.

God sent His word to Joseph by an angel. We, on the other hand, have His word in a book that's always there to be opened, read, believed, and obeyed.

Joseph's life was in shambles. His dream of happiness and peace destroyed. His hopes for the future gone. In that distressing situation, God's word came to Joseph. And what message did God have for a man dealing with such an earth-shaking, devastating life situation? "Don't be afraid, I'm very much in control and I'm here to put your life back together again. No, things are not working out the way you planned and hoped, but they are working out exactly as I planned and directed. Mary has not been unfaithful. I have worked a miracle of a new creation in her body. Beyond your wildest dreams and fondest hopes, there is better news. She will bear the Messiah, and you have been chosen to be His earthly father."

In the midst of our own chaotic lives and broken dreams, God's message of Christmas speaks the same comfort and the same hope. Yes, life is both very real and very painful and intimidating at times, but Jesus Christ has come into the world to save sinners and to give life a depth and joy of meaning that no earthly combination of circumstances can ever produce or take away. "Fear not, Joseph. God is in control. Have faith, Joseph, and believe His word. Act wisely, Joseph, for you have your part in fulfilling God's plan. You have a choice, Joseph. You can believe God's word and direct your life in obedience, or you can miss out on all God has for you. Which will it be, Joseph? Make your choice."

What about it, men? How do you stack up with Joseph? What would you have done? In fact, what are you doing now to show that you are an obedient servant of God, a loving husband and father to your family?

How I love those next words! How they challenge me and bring tears of repentance and shame. "Then Joseph arose and did as the angel of the Lord commanded him and took Mary as his wife." What a tragedy for him and for the rest of the world if Joseph had not obeyed the word of God. Little do we realize what grief we bring on ourselves and many others every time we fail to hear and do God's bidding.

In time, when everything was in place, they came to Bethlehem, the city of the great king, and there Jesus was born. But the story does not end there. Angels sang, shepherds came on the night of His birth, and later the lordly wise men came, too. All of them bore witness to the truth Joseph received and believed. But the coming of the wise men brought trouble of which Joseph knew not, nor could have known until it was too late. While Joseph peacefully slept in quiet little Bethlehem, a murderous plot was being carried out. Herod's death squad was marching towards Bethlehem with orders to kill all little boy babies two years old and under. There was no escape!

II. Joseph and the Angel: Act 2

Yes, Mary's child is the Messiah. One day, He will rule the whole of creation, but just then He was a helpless little boy who was destined for death. But not this night, for once more God sent His word to Joseph by an angel. Last time, it had been a comforting word, an assuring word, a guiding word. This time, it was a warning word, a word of protection from danger and death.

"Arise," said the angel, "and take the Child and His mother and flee to Egypt, and remain there until I tell you; for Herod is going to search for the Child to destroy Him." Joseph awoke with a fright in a cold sweat. "Maybe it was that pizza with green peppers I ate last night," he could have thought. "A nightmare, nothing more," he could have said. But instead, he remembered how God's word had rescued his life from despair; now by God's word, the little son's life would be spared.

How often we may find ourselves in situations of great danger. I don't mean the common dangers we all face living in a fallen world under the curse of Eden, but the more deadly dangers of temptation and sin that lead to eternal death. God's book is filled with words of warning, all too often ignored. "In the day you sin, you will surely die," God warned; but Adam would not listen.

To brooding, angry Cain, God warned, "Sin is crouching at your door, but you must master it." He did not and his own brother lay dead at his feet in a pool of blood. The books of Israel's history, Proverbs, the prophetic writings, the Ten Commandments, the Sermon on the Mount, and all the epistles — not to mention Revelation — contain God's timely words of warning. "In the day that you sin you will surely die." These words, in essence, sum up all the warnings from God's Word. Alas, that we so often and stubbornly ignore them, to our hurt and detriment. Joseph listened, Joseph obeyed, and in the middle of the night roused his young family out of bed and made a hasty flight to Egypt. At dawn, Herod's soldiers arrived in Bethlehem to kill the babies, but Jesus was safely on his way to Egypt in His mother's arms and in good Joseph's obedience to

God's word. What a protection to wrap around your children! How they need it!

There, they settled down to live awhile, and Joseph watched over his family and provided for them as a good father should. But it was not God's plan for Jesus to grow up in a foreign land.

III. Joseph's Last Encounter with the Angel

First a word of comfort, then a word of warning, now a word of guidance and hope. Once more, and for the last time, we learn of Joseph and his angelic dreams. "Arise and take the young Child and His mother and go into the land of Israel, for they are dead who sought the Child's life." (Ah, what a great truth; what a comfort, what hope.) "Go where God leads you, Joseph, and trust His loving care."

God's word guided Joseph in all his important decisions. It offers the same to us: comfort, guidance, warning, and hope. What more could you ask of the Bible? So, Joseph went back home again; first to Judea, but then on back to Galilee, to his home town of Nazareth where Jesus grew to manhood.

This is almost the last we ever hear of Joseph before he faded into obscurity. What a godly man! What an example of trust and obedience! What an earthly father to raise God's Son! What a blessing awaits us when we meet him in heaven and with him worship Emmanuel, the Wonderful Counselor, the Mighty God, the Everlasting Father, the Prince of Peace; Joseph's Lord and ours, Jesus Christ.

Unto Us A Boy is Born

Brightly

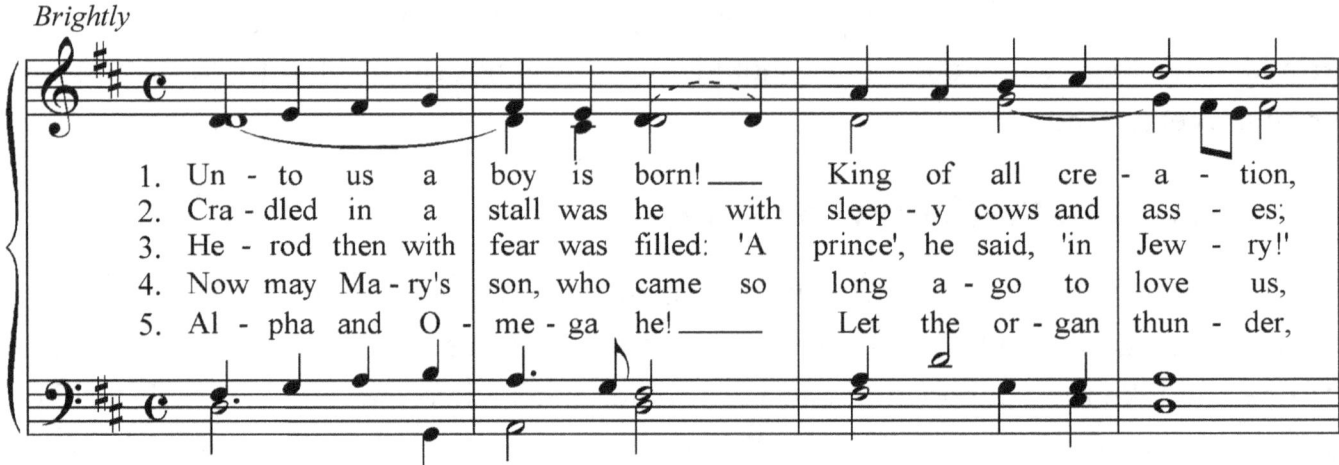

1. Un-to us a boy is born! King of all cre-a-tion,
2. Cra-dled in a stall was he with sleep-y cows and ass-es;
3. He-rod then with fear was filled: 'A prince', he said, 'in Jew-ry!'
4. Now may Ma-ry's son, who came so long a-go to love us,
5. Al-pha and O-me-ga he! Let the or-gan thun-der,

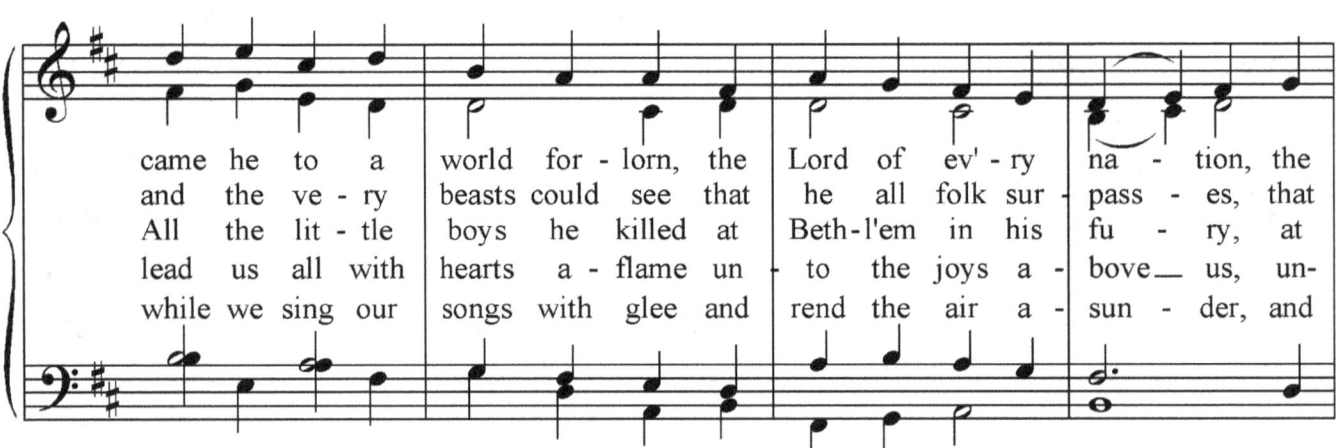

came he to a world for-lorn, the Lord of ev'-ry na-tion, the
and the ve-ry beasts could see that he all folk sur-pass-es, that
All the lit-tle boys he killed at Beth-l'em in his fu-ry, at
lead us all with hearts a-flame un-to the joys a-bove us, un-
while we sing our songs with glee and rend the air a-sun-der, and

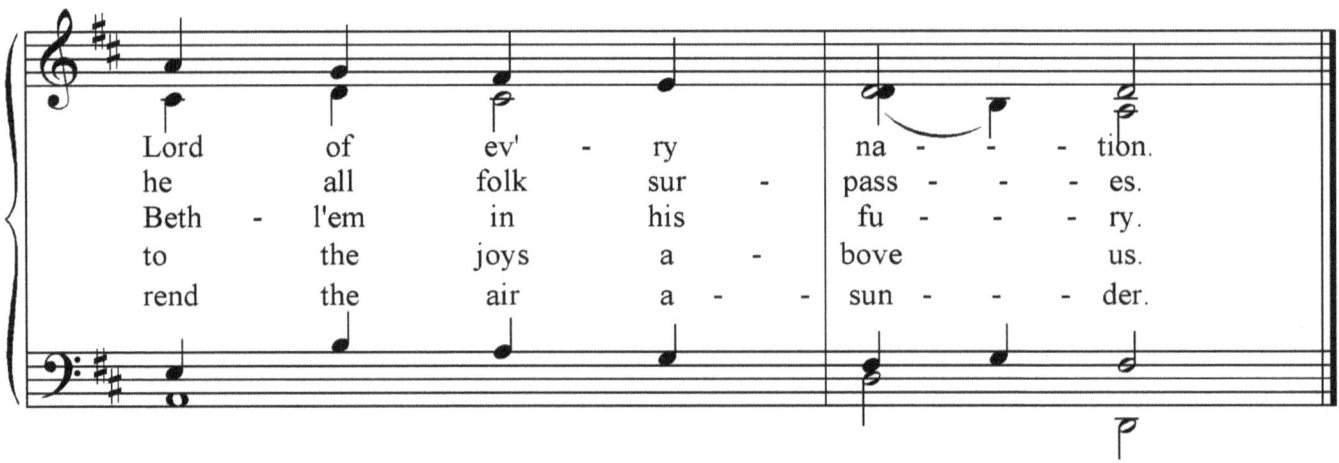

Lord of ev'-ry na-tion.
he all folk sur-pass-es.
Beth-l'em in his fu-ry.
to the joys a-bove us.
rend the air a-sun-der.

Words: Anonymous, 15th century Latin; trans. Percy Dearmer (1867-1936), 1928
Music: from *Piæ Cantiones*, 15th century

Tune: *Puer nobis nascitur*

Hymn Notes

This carol is a loose translation of the well-known Latin hymn *Puer Nobis Nascitur*. The earliest discovered instance of the hymn in print was found in a 14th century German manuscript called *The Moosburg Gradual*. This is a collection of songs derived from 12th and 13th century liturgical books, which suggests that the carol was in existence considerably earlier than the 14th century. It might be of interest to note that all of the carols printed in *The Moosburg Gradual* were recorded in 1997 by a choral ensemble called Niederaltaicher Scholaren. The group is based in Germany and specializes in music of the Middle Ages.

This hymn is also found the *Piae Cantiones,* a book of 74 sacred and secular Latin songs of medieval Europe. The contents were assembled by Swedish Lutheran cleric Jaakko Suomalainen and published in Sweden through the efforts of T.P. Rutha, a Finnish Catholic student. *Unto us a boy is born* had been in existence 200 years or more when it was printed in this 1582 collection.

The *Piae Cantiones* is an historic collection because of the insight that it provides into the culture of the era. It is significant, too, in the simple fact that it kept the songs from falling out of use. There have been regular reprints of the collection and occasional additions to its contents over the centuries. It remains available for sale, and many of its songs continue in use today. The Christmas hymns *Personent hodie* (*On this day, earth shall ring*) and *Gaudete (Rejoice)* are in many hymnals and are often heard in churches and concerts during the Christmas season. Their driving, jubilant rhythms have inspired many composers through the ages to make choral arrangements of them.

The text of *Unto us a boy is born* is distinct from the majority of other Christmas carols in that it includes in its recitation of the Christmas story Herod's plot to kill the Christ Child. That, too, is the reason for its inclusion in this chapter.

Percy Dearmer, translator of this text, was born in London in 1867. He was ordained in the Church of England in 1892, earned a Master of Arts degree from Christ Church, Oxford in 1896, and served several brief pastorates before beginning a 14-year term as vicar of St. Mary the Virgin at Primrose Hill, London. During World War I, he served as chaplain to the British Red Cross in Serbia. It was there that his first wife, Mabel, died of a fever. After the war, he served as Canon of Westminster, and, from 1919 until his death in 1936, as professor of Ecclesiastical Art at King's College London. He authored many books and pamphlets on church art and history, and was editor of the hymnal *Songs of Praise* (1931). He might be best known for his exceedingly popular *The Parson's Handbook,* a liturgical manual for Anglican priests, and for his work as the editor of *The English Hymnal,* which developed into an authoritative collection second only to *Hymns Ancient and Modern.*

Dearmer was a self-described socialist who had a heart for social justice. He teamed with Ralph Vaughan Williams and Martin Shaw to edit the *Oxford Book of Carols* (1928), and to effect the revival and spread of traditional and medieval English musical forms. Many of the books that he wrote had as their topic such subject matters as history, ecclesiastical arts, and social issues. A sampling of titles includes: Christian Socialism and Practical Christianity (1897), The English Liturgy (1903), Socialism and Religion (1908), The Church and Social Questions (1910), and Reunion and Rome (1911).

Dearmer died suddenly at his home in 1936. His remains are buried in the north cloister of Westminster Abbey in London.

- TW

The Adoration of the Shepherds

Mattia Preti (1613-1699), Italy

Oil on canvas

Creative Commons, licensed under CC BY 2.0

This rendering of the shepherds' adoration of the newborn Messiah is brimming with detail, emotion, and humanity. Note the varied postures and the range of expressions on the faces of the shepherds … awe and wonder, bewilderment, joy, contentment. The muted colors and soft edges draw the viewer into the scene such that one can almost smell the odors permeating the cave and feel the warmth emanating from the animals' bodies and buffering the chill. Note, too, the posture of the animals, the tenderness of Mary and Joseph, and the angel trailing a banner just outside the entry to the cave. (Might the banner read, "Glory to God in the highest"?) Such expressiveness, drama, and movement are characteristic of Renaissance art.

We Hear the Christmas Angels, Their Great Glad Tidings Tell
Part 4: "Unto Certain Poor Shepherds"

And in the same region there were shepherds out in the field, keeping watch over their flock by night. ⁹And an angel of the Lord appeared to them, and the glory of the Lord shone around them, and they were filled with great fear. ¹⁰And the angel said to them, "Fear not, for behold, I bring you good news of great joy that will be for all the people. ¹¹For unto you is born this day in the city of David a Savior, who is Christ the Lord. ¹²And this will be a sign for you: you will find a baby wrapped in swaddling cloths and lying in a manger." ¹³And suddenly there was with the angel a multitude of the heavenly host praising God and saying, ¹⁴"Glory to God in the highest, and on earth peace among those with whom he is pleased!" ¹⁵When the angels went away from them into heaven, the shepherds said to one another, "Let us go over to Bethlehem and see this thing that has happened, which the Lord has made known to us." ¹⁶And they went with haste and found Mary and Joseph, and the baby lying in a manger. ¹⁷And when they saw it, they made known the saying that had been told them concerning this child. ¹⁸And all who heard it wondered at what the shepherds told them. ¹⁹But Mary treasured up all these things, pondering them in her heart. ²⁰And the shepherds returned, glorifying and praising God for all they had heard and seen, as it had been told them.

- Luke 2:8-20

It is impossible for us to understand the tremendous effect of the great German reformer Martin Luther on the late medieval world. He almost single-handedly broke forever the spiritual stranglehold the corrupt medieval church held on the western world. His birth and ministry coincided with the opening of the Americas to exploration and colonization. His teaching and preaching laid the foundation for the whole Reformation in all its many forms and branches.

But Luther was not only a great leader and theologian, he was also a very human person. He married, had children, and pastored a church. He loved to preach to the common man for, as he once boasted, "I am a peasant's son; my father, grandfather, and all my ancestors were genuine peasants." He also said his mother carried wood from the forest on her back, "and father and mother worked their flesh off their bones to bring up seven children."

He never lost his concern and love for the common man, and his preaching was usually couched in the language of the common man of his day, even sometimes with crude and street language; not vulgarities, but not far from this. As a family man and a small parish pastor, he especially loved Christmas and to preach Christmas sermons. He wrote songs and plays for children to sing and act out at Christmas, and often let his own imagination fill in the details omitted by Scripture.

For this Christmas Eve service, I have carefully worked through Luther's sermon about the shepherds, and, as nearly as possible and appropriate, I will preach the same sermon he preached almost five hundred years ago. Like Luther, use your imagination and try to picture the scene as this great but common man shared the wonder and joy of the shepherds as they heard "the Christmas angels, their great glad tidings tell."

※

" 'And there were in the same country shepherds abiding in the field, keeping watch over their flock by night.' That was a mean job, watching flocks by night. Common sense calls it a low-down work, and the men who do it are regarded as trash. But Luke lauds the angels because they proclaimed their message only to shepherds watching their flock by night. These were real sheep herders. And what did they do? They did what shepherds should do. They stayed in their station and did the work of their calling. They were pure in heart and content with their work, not aspiring to be townsmen or nobles, nor envious of the mighty. Next to faith, this is the highest art — to be content with the calling in which God has placed you. I have not learned it yet.

"Who would have thought that men whose job was tending unreasoning animals would be so praised that not a pope nor a bishop is worthy to hand them a cup of water? It is the devil's work that no one wants to follow the shepherds. The married man wants to be without a wife, or the noble wants to be a prince. It is: 'If I were this! If I were that!' Foolish one, the best job is the one you have. If you are married, you cannot have a higher status. If you are a servant, you are in the best position. Be diligent and know that there are no greater saints on earth than servants. Do not say, 'If I were'; say 'I am.' A maiden who is always saying to herself, "If I were only someone else" will end up with a bad husband.

"Look at the shepherds. They were watching their flock by night and an angel came and made them apostles, prophets, and children of God. Caiaphas, Herod, and the high priests were not deemed worthy. I would rather be one of those shepherds than that the pope would make me a saint or the emperor.

"'And lo, the Angel of the Lord came upon them, and the glory of the Lord shone round about them, and they were sore afraid.' The field was flooded with light — brilliant, dazzling. Not the town, but the field was lighted up. Why did not the angels go to Jerusalem? There was worship established by God. There were the princes of the people and rulers in Church and state. There were the temple and the high priests ordained of God. Why did not the angel go to them? He went to Bethlehem, a dung heap compared with Jerusalem. And He did not go to the town of Bethlehem, but to the shepherds.

" 'And the angel said unto them, fear not: for behold, I bring you good tidings of great joy which shall be to all people.' This joy is not just for Peter and Paul, but for all people. Not just to apostles, prophets, and martyrs, but to you God says, 'Come see the baby Jesus.' 'Fear not,' said the angel. I fear death, the judgment of God, the world, hunger, and the like. The angel announces a Savior who will free us from fear. Not a word is said about our merits and works, but only the gift we are to receive.

" 'For unto you is born this day,' that is, unto us. For our sakes, He has taken flesh and blood from a woman that His birth might become our birth. I, too, may boast that I am a son of Mary. This is the way to observe Christmas — that Christ be formed in us. It is not enough that we should hear His story if the heart be closed. I must listen not to a history, but to a gift. If I tell you someone on a certain mountain has found a pile of gold, you will say, "What is that to me?" But if you are the one who found it, you will be joyful. What is it to me if someone else has goods, honor, riches, and a pretty wife? That does not touch the heart. But if you hear that Christ is yours, that takes root and a man becomes suddenly so strong that to him death and life are the same.

" 'And this shall be a sign unto you; you will find the babe wrapped in swaddling clothes, lying in a manger.' This is God's wedding. Where is the castle? A cow stall, a manger with an ox and ass — a fine bridal bed, fit to lay a dog in! But the angels are not ashamed of it. 'Ye shall find Him lying in a manger.' The only present you need to bring to this wedding is a happy heart. God smiles and all the hosts of heaven rejoice. 'And suddenly there was with the angel a multitude of the heavenly host.' An innumerable multitude. There are more angels in heaven than all the blades of grass in the whole world. They outnumber all who have ever lived on earth. You would think that some of the angels might have gone to baby Jesus to take Him a golden cradle or a feather bed, or at least some warm water. Why didn't they? They were singing that He was Lord and Savior. This is something we cannot understand and will have to wait til the resurrection to find out.

"They were 'praising God and saying, "Glory to God in the Highest." ' See what God did in heaven about this birth that the world despised and did not see and know. The joy was so great that the angels could not stay in heaven, but had to break out and tell man on earth. The angels proclaimed to the shepherds, 'Tidings of great joy.' This is a great comfort to us. What the world despised the angels honored. They would have had a much bigger celebration if God had allowed them, but He wished to teach us through His Son to despise the pomp of this world.

"All the angels in heaven, not one excepted, sang, 'Glory to God in the highest.' What a shame that all men should not preach this word when all the angels in heaven play it on pipes and organs for all eternity. The angels had no bigger congregation than two shepherds in a field. They were filled with too great joy for words. And we who hear this message seldom feel a spark of joy. I hate myself when I see Him laid in a manger, hear the angels sing, but my heart does not leap into flame. We should all despise ourselves when we remain so cold to this good news. We act as if it were only a cold historical fact that does not touch our hearts.

"They sang, 'And on earth peace, good will towards man.' The kingdom of Christ is a proclamation of peace and grace, for the angels sang that He was the Savior of the world, to free His people and save them from their sin. This He has done and is still doing. He is not the sort of king who fights with a sword. Rather, He rules with the gracious preaching of peace. For this reason, He is called Jesus, Savior. This is a dear and precious comfort to troubled and tormented consciences laden with sin. He has come to bring life, not death. These are not the words of man. This is preaching from heaven and, God be praised, as we hear it or read it, is just he same as if we heard the angels.

"The shepherds did not see the angels; they only saw a great light, and heard the words of the angel. We, too, see a great light and hear their message if our hearts are open to it."

Angels We Have Heard On High

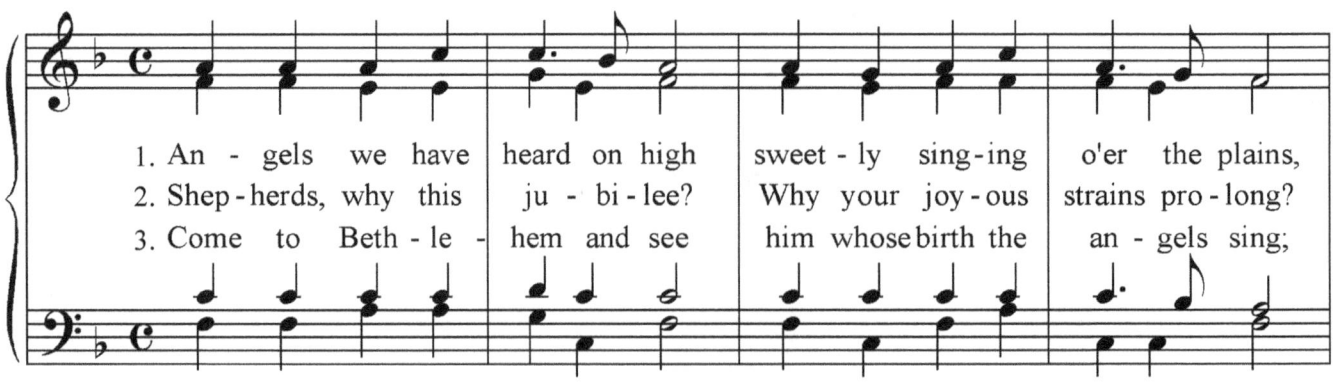

1. An-gels we have heard on high sweet-ly sing-ing o'er the plains, and the moun-tains in re-ply ech-o back their joy-ous strains.
2. Shep-herds, why this ju-bi-lee? Why your joy-ous strains pro-long? Say what may the tid-ings be, which in-spire your heav'n-ly song?
3. Come to Beth-le-hem and see him whose birth the an-gels sing; come, a-dore on bend-ed knee Christ the Lord, the new-born King.

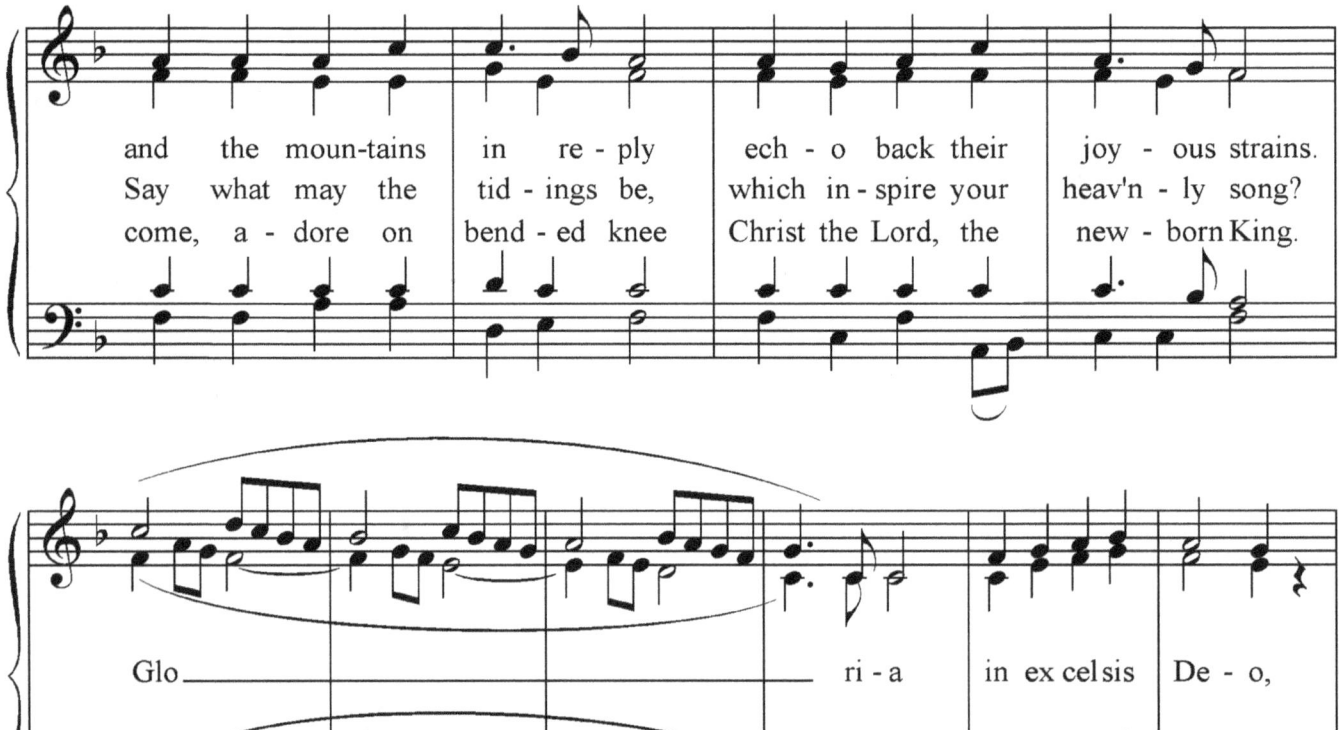

Glo — — — ri-a in ex cel sis De-o,

Words: Traditional French carol, 18th century; trans. James Chadwick (1813-1882), 1860
Music: Traditional French melody, 18th century; arr. Edward Barnes (1887-1958)

Tune: *Gloria*

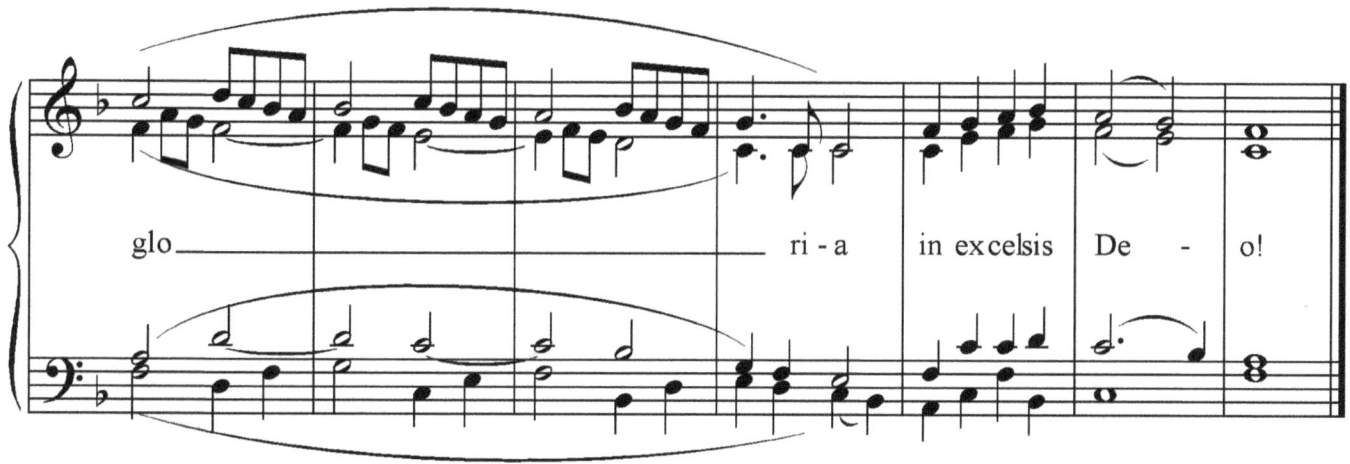

Hymn Notes

This carol comes to us from 18th century France, possibly from the Lorraine region, an area in northeast France that borders Belgium. Beyond that jot of information, nothing exists to shine a light upon its origin. Its first publication has traced to an 1842 French collection titled, *Choix de cantiques sur des airs nouveaux (Selected hymns with new tunes)*. It appeared in eight stanzas.

Many English translations of the text are in existence. The first is believed to have been made by James Montgomery in 1816 and published in his newspaper, the *Sheffield Iris*. (See Hymn Notes, page 47.) His translation would end up being the frame for *Angels from the realms of glory*. The translation used most often today was made by James Chadwick in 1860 and adapted for use by Henri Hémy in 1862. Most modern hymnals use three of the carol's eight stanzas, although a few add a fourth — usually "See Him in a manger laid, / Whom the choirs of angels praise; / Mary, Joseph, lend your aid, / While our hearts in love we raise." This carol is one that requires caution when singing it from a hymnal other than your own, if you want to avoid singing the wrong words in your neighbor's ear. Due to the many translations available, and the many differences among those translations, there are quite a few text variances from hymnal to hymnal.

James Chadwick was born in 1813 in Drogheda, Ireland. After his ordination to the priesthood in 1836, he served for three years as general prefect at his alma mater, Ushaw College. Over the next 13 years, he taught humanities and philosophy at the college. His rise through academia continued in 1849 when he became vice-president of the college, professor of dogmatic theology, and, later, professor of pastoral theology. He was elected bishop of the diocese in 1866 and served in that office for 16 years. For one year during that period, he also served as president of Ushaw College. According to an article at www.catholic.org, Chadwick was "a man of great personal dignity and charm" who "is remembered for his meekness and sweetness of manner." In addition to a large body of pastoral letters and smaller publications on Catholic doctrine, his works include *Saint Teresa's Own Words: Instructions on the Prayer of Recollection* (Newcastle, 1878) and *Instructions How to Meditate* (published anonymously). He dabbled in hymnody only fleetingly: he is credited with authoring only three hymns, and *Angels we have heard on high* is his sole translation.

The carol's anonymous tune, like the text, has been traced to 18th century France. The arrangement used in many contemporary hymnals is by Edward Shippen Barnes (1887-1958). Barnes was an American organist who studied at Yale University and then at the Schola Cantorum in Paris (See Hymn Notes, page 105.) After completing his sojourn in Paris, he returned to the United States to assume the position of organist at the Church of the Incarnation in New York, followed by like positions at Rutgers Presbyterian Church, also in New York; Saint Stephen's Church in Philadelphia; and First Presbyterian Church in Santa Monica, CA.

The Latin text *Gloria in excelsis Deo* means "glory to God in the highest."

- TW

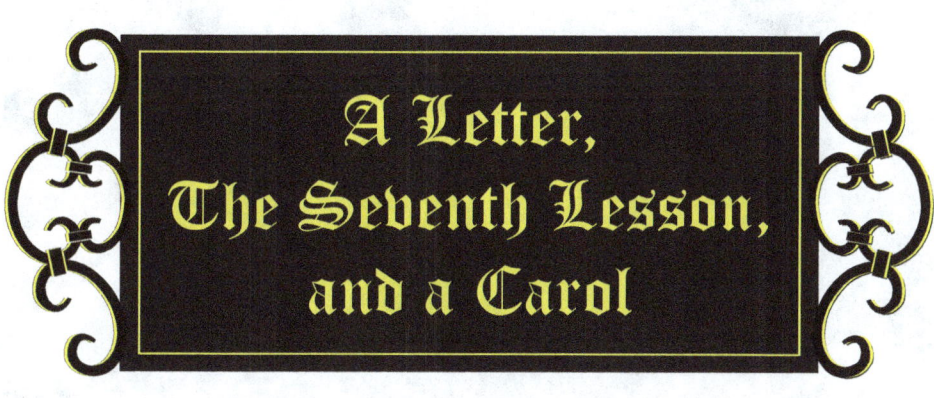

The Annunciation to the Shepherds, ca. 1555/1560

Jacopo Bassano (ca. 1510-1592), Italy

Oil on canvas

National Gallery of Art Open Access Collection

Dramatic expressiveness is again on display in this further example of Renaissance painting. However, the artist has put his own mark on it through a variation in the representation of the biblical story. Instead of the typical small group of shepherds on a vast plain, Bassano gives us a family of Shepherds in what appears to be a comfortably sheltered area. The landscape is an area in his native Dolomite region of northern Italy.

God's Messengers

Dearly Beloved,

Believe it or not, Christmas is just around the next turn of the calendar! This is the time of year when we have an opportunity to tell the world about the angels of Christmas and all the wondrous stories they came to tell. Maybe, just maybe, we can convince people that our stories and our great story are real and true. But angels are no longer God's messengers to convey His revelation of peace on earth, good will towards men. That task has been assigned to people who believe that God's Son, the Lord Jesus Christ has come to earth and brought God's salvation to mankind.

When the Lord Jesus had completed His work on earth before He went back to heaven, He told His disciples to go into all the world and preach the Good News to all people around the whole wide world. That is still His command and will be until He returns to earth again to establish the New Creation.

God had frequently used angels to bring His message to His chosen people. The place of angels in bringing God's revelation in the Old Testament was very prominent. And when God would send His Son into the world, He assigned His angels to bring that news to the parents of John the Baptist and tell them their son would be the herald of the coming Messiah.

An angel came to the Virgin Mary to inform her that she would bear a son, though still a young and chaste virgin, and that His conception would be a mighty miracle of the Holy Spirit. When Mary's espoused husband, Joseph, was troubled at this news, God sent an angel to calm his troubled heart and convince him that Mary had been true to him and was with child by the Holy Spirit. The angels stayed in touch with Joseph to warn and instruct him how to escape King Herod's attempt to kill the infant Jesus, telling him to flee into Egypt.

At the time of His birth, angels were sent to certain poor shepherds to announce the birth of Jesus in Bethlehem. Then, the angels went back to heaven and only made a very few appearances after that. We are told they are now ministering spirits to aid and comfort the elect. That seems to be their primary role until Jesus comes back again in glorious triumph with all His saints and myriads of mighty angels.

So, the role of spreading the Good News is no longer assigned to angels, but is in the hands of those who believe: ordinary people like you and me. Have you told anyone lately that "God so loved the world that He gave His only begotten Son that whosoever believes in Him should not perish but have everlasting life"? If not, why not? What could be a better time than now, and especially this close to Christmas Day?

God grant you a blessed Christmas and joyful, useful New Year.

Love and prayers,

Gordon and Miriam Reed

After the Angels Leave

> And in the same region there were shepherds out in the field, keeping watch over their flock by night. ⁹And an angel of the Lord appeared to them, and the glory of the Lord shone around them, and they were filled with great fear. ¹⁰And the angel said to them, "Fear not, for behold, I bring you good news of great joy that will be for all the people. ¹¹For unto you is born this day in the city of David a Savior, who is Christ the Lord. ¹²And this will be a sign for you: you will find a baby wrapped in swaddling cloths and lying in a manger." ¹³And suddenly there was with the angel a multitude of the heavenly host praising God and saying, ¹⁴"Glory to God in the highest, and on earth peace among those with whom he is pleased!" ¹⁵When the angels went away from them into heaven, the shepherds said to one another, "Let us go over to Bethlehem and see this thing that has happened, which the Lord has made known to us." ¹⁶And they went with haste and found Mary and Joseph, and the baby lying in a manger. ¹⁷And when they saw it, they made known the saying that had been told them concerning this child. ¹⁸And all who heard it wondered at what the shepherds told them. ¹⁹But Mary treasured up all these things, pondering them in her heart. ²⁰And the shepherds returned, glorifying and praising God for all they had heard and seen, as it had been told them.
>
> *- Luke 2:8-20*

Can you believe it? Christmas is already over. It came with a rush and vanished even more rapidly. I always want time to stand still for just a little while. The calendar is so packed with events; the demands of shopping, wrapping, and mailing are so insistent. The programs and the parties come with such rapidity. Then, all of a sudden, it's Christmas morning and before long the presents are all opened, many have already taken down the tree, and it's soon back to school, back to work, and of course there is tomorrow morning when everyone rushes to the store to exchange unwanted gifts, wrong colors and sizes. People are almost as mean and ugly then as they are that silly mob scene the day after Thanksgiving. Christmas seems to vanish in a frenzy of ill will. For far too many people, Christmas only means people who really can't afford it spending money on gifts other people don't really need.

Doesn't it leave you with a bad taste and a let-down feeling? Good news! It doesn't have to be that way. In fact, you can hold on to the true Christmas forever and never let it go if you really try. Let's join the shepherds in the fields near Bethlehem, and they will tell you how.

I. The Sudden and Unexpected Visit from Heaven

These words, "And there were in the same country shepherds abiding in the fields, keeping watch over their flock by night ..." sound so much more romantic and adventuresome than it really was. These men were nomads. They lived in tents right out there among the sheep. Camping out can be fun only if you know it's for a short time, and then you can come back home and take a shower and sleep in a warm bed. It wasn't like that for the shepherds. That's how they lived. That's what abiding in the fields really means. Life was boring, dirty, exhausting, dangerous, and unrewarding.

Then in one glorious night, one glory filled moment, everything changed. God's angel came to these men with news so astounding, so life changing, that they were filled with awe and wonder. "Unto you is born this day in the city of David, a Savior, who is Christ the Lord." Then, as if to make sure they understood, suddenly the lone angel was joined by myriads, thousands upon thousands, whose voices thundered and echoed across the Judean hills, "GLORY TO GOD IN THE HIGHEST, AND ON EARTH PEACE, GOOD WILL TOWARDS MEN." In a way, that's how Christmas happens every year. The New Year begins, rushes swiftly by, and suddenly it's Christmas again. We hear the old familiar carols; ten thousand lights appear everywhere as if by magic; trees, real and otherwise, spring up in a million homes, all decorated and beautiful; and, for the most part, people act kindly towards each other, briefly. Why, it's almost as if the angels have come among us again.

II. The Sudden and Disappointing Departure

Just as suddenly as they came, they were gone; gone as if they had never even been there at all. So, there the shepherds are. It's all dark again. The fire has burned low and the sheep are still there. So, now what? The angels have gone back to heaven, the decorations back to the closet, the trees to the dumpster, and the misfitting presents back to the store. Christmas is over, back to work Monday, old problems hang on and new ones crop up. It is sometimes easier to identify with the shepherds right after the angels went away than while they were surrounded by the heavenly host. "No one will believe us!" they might have said. "We have our work to do," they could have said. But what they did say enshrines them in our hearts forever, and points the way for us to experience the joy of the Lord and the true wonder of Christmas forever.

III. Salvaging Christmas

"Let us now go, even unto Bethlehem, and see this thing which has come to pass, which the Lord has made known unto us." The one thing which was so overwhelming to the shepherds was not that they had seen and heard angels, but rather that God had made something wonderful known. Angels come and go, but God's Word abides forever.

Christmases come and then go, but the message which God revealed at Christmas is not confined to a few days at the end of each year. The message of Christmas is God's Word for all seasons. If you believe as the shepherds did that what they heard came as God's revelation of truth, angels — real or fanciful — are mere trappings of what is truly transcendent. Just as we may obscure the beauty of a tree with too many decorations, so we may dim the glory of Christmas with too many human trappings.

Never forget that the message of Christmas is the central theme of the whole Bible from Genesis to Revelation, beautifully summed up in these words, "God was in Christ, reconciling the world unto Himself, not imputing their trespasses to them, and has committed unto us the word of reconciliation."

Revelation requires faith. Granted that faith is a gift, but a gift to be received and put into action. What a perfect response of faith we find expressed in these words: "Let us now go and see this thing which the Lord has made known unto us." That is faith's beginning, but the journey is a lifetime of "going to Bethlehem and seeing" what the Lord has made known. It is a long road from justification to glorification. The path is called sanctification, and you must travel down many paths from Genesis through Revelation to really see what the Lord has made known unto you. What a tragedy that so many believers are content to remain weak and small in faith, unable to cope with the trials and tragedies of life, when all the while there is available and open before your eyes the complete and totally sufficient revelation of God — the Bible — just waiting for you to "go now even unto Bethlehem and see this thing which has come to pass, which the Lord has made known."

And for those who make this lifetime journey, exploring every line and word of God's Word, "strength they find to meet their trials here; trusting in their Father's wise bestowments, they've no cause for worry or for fear." When overtaken by grief, they are comforted by the God of all comfort. When perplexed, yet they are not in despair. When opposed and persecuted, they sing their midnight songs of praise, for they are never forsaken. They do not lose heart, for though the outward man perish, the inner man is being renewed day by day.

So the shepherds searched, and so they found, and so they rejoiced. But there was one more thing the message of Christmas demanded of them. "Now when they had seen Him, they made widely known the saying which was told them concerning this Child, then they returned, glorifying and praising God." They were still shepherds, but they were shepherds who had seen the Savior, Christ the Lord, and they would never be the same again. Once you know Him, truly known Him, you must follow that path, too.

Making "widely known" what we have been shown and what we have experienced in Christ becomes a way of life.

That's how you hold on to Christmas after the angels go back to heaven; you give it away. No, that's not quite it; say, rather, you give yourself away by gladly sharing Christ and the message of salvation with those God brings across your path. Even more, following the Good Shepherd, we go seeking the lost that the Holy Spirit may bring them to Christ, and that they, too, may glorify and praise God for the great and precious gift of His Son, our Lord.

Yes, angels played their part in the story of Christmas, and they helped to tell that story, but, after all, it is the story itself — of the Incarnation — that is the heart and soul of Christmas, and that story is never ending, and is the source of our never failing joy. So what if you never see an angel at Christmas or any other time; you have seen something far more wonderful: the complete, perfect, glorious revelation of God, and that the heart of that revelation is the One of whom the shepherds said, "Let us now go and see this thing which has come to pass, which the Lord has made known unto us."

Yes, God sent His angels from heaven to announce the birth of His Son. But before Jesus went back to heaven, He commissioned His disciples — which includes everyone who confesses Him — to announce and proclaim the good news of salvation to a lost and dying world. You are doing that … aren't you?

Hark! the Herald Angels Sing

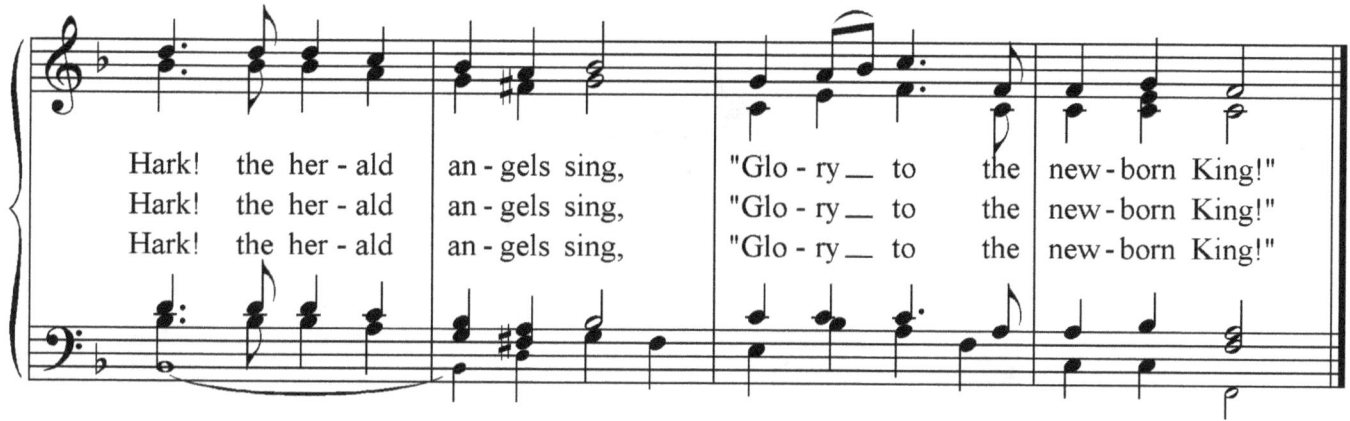

Words: Charles Wesley (1707-1788), 1739
Music: Felix Mendelssohn (1809-1847), 1840; arr., William F. Cummings (1831-1915), 1856

Tune: *Mendelssohn*

Hymn Notes

Charles Wesley, cofounder of Methodism and arguably one of the greatest hymn writers of all time, wrote this joyous statement of Incarnation theology within a year of his spiritual conversion. Wesley does not simply tell the story of Christ's birth in this hymn; he infuses the text with the "why" of His birth. The answer is first seen in the second line of the first stanza: "God and sinners reconciled," and again in the third stanza with "born that man no more may die." Wesley addresses the "who" of Jesus' nature in strong theological language: "Veiled in flesh the Godhead see" and "hail th'incarnate Deity" and "mild he lays his glory by." Through this approach to his telling of the story, Wesley covers Christ's birth, ministry, and salvific purpose in one broad sweep, thereby providing a succinct statement of the crux of the Gospel message.

The *Psalter Hymnal Handbook* offers this summary exegesis of the hymn: "A curious mixture of exclamation, exhortation, and theological reflection. The focus shifts rapidly from angels, to us, to nations. The text's strength may not lie so much in any orderly sequence of thought but in its use of Scripture to teach its theology. That teaching surely produces in us a childlike response of faith; we too can sing 'Glory to the newborn King!'"

When Wesley published the hymn in 1739, the opening lines read,

> Hark, how all the welkin [heavens] rings
> Glory to the King of Kings.

George Whitefield, the charismatic evangelist who was a key player in the Protestant revival in America and influential in Charles Wesley's conversion, changed these lines to "Hark! the herald angels sing" and published the text with additional alterations in 1753. The convention of repeating the opening phrase after each stanza started in 1782.

The hymn's tune came from the second movement of Felix Mendelssohn's *Festgesang*, a composition for male chorus and brass. *Festgesang* was first performed at the 1840 Gutenberg Festival in Leipzig, Germany that celebrated the anniversary of Gutenberg's invention of the printing press. William Cummings adapted the tune to match Wesley's text. Although Mendelssohn once insisted that the melody would never be an appropriate match to sacred music, its pairing with *Hark! The herald angels sing* in 1856 caused the hymn's popularity to soar.

If one reads the entries in Charles Wesley's journal immediately following his conversion, it will become clear that there could not have been a better match for this text than Mendelssohn's tune. It not only stands up to the strength of the words; it also conveys the irrepressible joy and conviction of faith that is evident in Wesley's journal entries.

- TW

A Letter, The Eighth Lesson, and a Carol

The Journey of the Magi, 1433-45

Stefano di Giovanni (ca. 1400-1450), Italy

Tempera and gold on wood

The Metropolitan Museum of Art Open Access Collection

This depiction of the three wise men journeying with their entourage to Bethlehem appears on a remnant of a large altarpiece titled, "Adoration of the Magi." The fur-lined hat worn by the wise man dressed in pink was inspired by a 1432 visit to Siena by King Sigismund of Hungary.

Stefano di Giovanni, also known as Sassetta, is considered to have been a leading painter of 15th century Siena. His work was pivotal in moving the Sienese painting tradition from the Gothic to Renaissance style.

A Devotional for Christmas 2009

The people who walked in darkness have seen a great light.
Those who dwell in the land of the shadow of death, upon them has a light shined. (Isaiah 9:2)

Dearly Beloved,

Great darkness loomed on the horizon of tiny Judah. The great and cruel Assyrian Empire had once more turned its hungry, greedy eyes southward to gaze upon Jerusalem with evil intent. Already, certain areas of Galilee had been submerged under this irresistible flood of conquest, and the gloom was spreading ever nearer the heart of Judah — the capital city, Jerusalem. There was no earthly power there to defend the Holy City against the invaders. But "the people who walked in darkness have seen a great light. Those who dwell in the land of the shadow of death, upon them has a light shined." The message proclaimed by Isaiah was a message of great hope.

The message of Christmas is a message of great hope. It is true that we are surrounded by a great darkness. There is great darkness within the heart and soul of America. In the lifetime of most of us, we have seen the decline — to the point of near disintegration — the foundations upon which our forebears built this land of freedom. The values which once were almost taken for granted are being dismissed with casual scorn. The claims of Christ and foundational truths of God's revealed Word are either ignored or angrily rejected. There is a great and growing darkness in the world. There are powerful forces of evil bent on the fall of this nation, and are the sworn enemies of Christ and His Kingdom.

But over this discouraging scene of darkness and apparent hopelessness a "great light" may still be seen with the eye of faith. The truth of the Incarnation of God the Son in the form of a tiny baby born in a manger is the focal point of that brilliant light. That seemingly helpless little baby boy was none other than the Lord of Glory of whom John said, "The Word was with God, and the Word was God. All things were made through Him ... And the Word was made flesh, and dwelt among us." For the infant of Bethlehem became the Christ of the cross and the empty tomb. His Gospel of grace will lead you into the everlasting kingdom of light, where no darkness will ever shine. Yes, we dwell in the "shadow of death," but our Lord Jesus offers life eternal to those who will come to His light. So Christians, look up, for God is looking down with His grace on those who love and follow His Son. In His good time, the present darkness will give way to everlasting light and life, and truly there will be "peace on earth, good will towards men."

Merry Christmas, and may God bless us every one.

Much love and many prayers,

Gordon and Miriam Reed

The Wise Men vs. Secular Humanism

> Now after Jesus was born in Bethlehem of Judea in the days of Herod the king, behold, wise men from the east came to Jerusalem, ² saying, "Where is he who has been born king of the Jews? For we saw his star when it rose and have come to worship him." ³ When Herod the king heard this, he was troubled, and all Jerusalem with him; ⁴ and assembling all the chief priests and scribes of the people, he inquired of them where the Christ was to be born. ⁵ They told him, "In Bethlehem of Judea, for so it is written by the prophet: ⁶ "'And you, O Bethlehem, in the land of Judah, are by no means least among the rulers of Judah; for from you shall come a ruler who will shepherd my people Israel.'" ⁷ Then Herod summoned the wise men secretly and ascertained from them what time the star had appeared. ⁸ And he sent them to Bethlehem, saying, "Go and search diligently for the child, and when you have found him, bring me word, that I too may come and worship him." ⁹ After listening to the king, they went on their way. And behold, the star that they had seen when it rose went before them until it came to rest over the place where the child was. ¹⁰ When they saw the star, they rejoiced exceedingly with great joy. ¹¹ And going into the house, they saw the child with Mary his mother, and they fell down and worshiped him. Then, opening their treasures, they offered him gifts, gold and frankincense and myrrh. ¹² And being warned in a dream not to return to Herod, they departed to their own country by another way.
>
> *- Matthew 2:1-12*

Even as Mary's life and actions challenge and defy the values of radical feminism, and Joseph's values reveal the empty philosophy of life as expressed in the modern "macho man," so the story of the wise men exposes the vain and empty claims of liberal humanism which have replaced Christian philosophy and ethics as the dominant cultural mindset in America and in the western civilization as a whole. Before I try to convince you that the wise men were truly the wise ones in this conflict, and the wisdom of the modern prophets of liberal humanism is worse than sheer folly, I will have to tell you who "they" are and some of the non-negotiables they adamantly insist are absolute truths about which there can be no arguments. I will do this not by trying to analyze their theories of truth and meaning, but by the consequences of their theories which have brought us to the brink of cultural and national suicide. I will have time to mention only a few of these, but enough, I hope, to convince you of my case.

I. Fools Who Call Themselves Wise

One of the places in which the folly of the so-called wise and sophisticated is most apparent may be found in the current educational establishment. Most, if not all, of the major universities which are widely acclaimed as the leading schools of educational philosophy and teacher training are firmly in the hands of radical leftists who are attempting, very successfully, to impose their non-values upon a gullible populace, replacing the traditional approaches to education which were based on biblical principles for the most part. These are people who seem to hate America and are determined to radicalize this nation. Neutral history disproves all their theories, so what do they do? They simply rewrite history, and fill the textbooks our children are forced to use with fancy and fabrication, and both with malicious intent!

Another example of this effort is seen in the propaganda used to change attitudes and values towards human sexuality. We were told a few years ago that if only the public schools were allowed to teach sex education from a non-Christian point of view, we would see a dramatic drop in such problems as sexually transmitted diseases and teen pregnancies. So we all said, "Sure, that sounds great," and we gave in. The results? 'Nuff said. Then when it became obvious that this wasn't working, we were told that here was no way to curb or inhibit or restrain sexual instincts in children and teens, so all we have to do is teach them how to have "safe sex." What a colossal failure that has been.

As for teaching moral values, holding people responsible for their actions, and exercising biblical discipline in the schools, or even in the home, this was thought to be wrong and unlawful, and yet we wonder why we are raising a generation which has little respect for parents or any other authority, for law and order, or even for human life. Dr. Spock, who was himself a miserable moral failure, was accepted by several generations of parents as being the infallible prophet of a new way of raising kids. Results? Look around you. Yet some people criticize those who send their children to Christian schools or home-school on the basis that their children would be deprived of social development. Please God, may they be deprived and spared the kind of social development the liberal establishment has in mind.

One final example of this attempt to undermine the Judeo-Christian foundation of this country would be the divorcing of scientific inquiry from the knowledge of God and the truth of creation. Some poor innocent souls still believe that the theory of evolution grew out of a neutral search for truth which led inevitably, on the basis of "scientific evidence," to the theory of evolution, now accepted by most people as indisputable fact. Nothing could be further from the truth. The theory of evolution grew directly out of a philosophy of atheism which had to explain the existence of the world and life apart from a Creator. What this has led to is the idea that man has evolved from lower life forms and is just another animal in the chain. So, we see the extremes in such things as "animal rights" movements. (The initials PETA could stand for "people eating tasty animals.")

The modern popular prophets and priests of this new religion called liberal humanism are drawn from Hollywood with its barnyard morality, and much of the media and the educational establishment. Sadly, they are financed by billions of dollars contributed to their upkeep by gullible people, many of whom are church members. Are you among their supporters? My point? So many people are looking for light and truth and meaning to life by walking into these "black holes" of eventual destruction, and which God has already condemned in His Word.

II. The Wise Men of Old and Their Search for Truth and Meaning

Who were these wise men who came seeking the infant Jesus? Many myths have been created to explain them. How many were there? No idea, except for the presentation of three gifts. What were their names? Still no answer. The legend that they were from India, China, and other mysterious Eastern empires has no basis in fact. There is a good deal of evidence to show they were from the Median-Persian and Babylonian empires, and this would tend to clear up the mystery and replace the legend with reliable and sober history.

They are called magi — a difficult, if not impossible, word to translate with accuracy or clarity. But the translation "wise men" is probably the most accurate, and is most descriptive of who these men were. The great Roman historian Herodotus reported the magi were originally a tribe of Medians in the Persian Empire. Once they were powerful and warlike. Politically ambitions, they attempted to seize control of the empire but their efforts failed and their power came to an end.

As the years passed, they turned their emphasis in other directions and became great scholars and priests. In some parts of the world, no offerings could be made to the gods unless one of their order was present. They were also trained in medicine and other sciences, especially astronomy. They were students of philosophy and were constantly seeking after truth. That they were deeply influenced by the Jews in captivity is apparent. Most likely, good Daniel and his godly friends, who were trained in all the arts and sciences of the Babylonians and also served in the court of the Persian conquerors, were the ones who acquainted them with the sacred writings of the Hebrew prophets, and especially the prophecies of the eventual coming of the great King of the whole world.

Based on these established facts, from here on we have to fill in the blanks with reasonable conjecture. By what means these astronomers knew a star was guiding them to Judea to seek for the great "King of the Jews" (and of all people) we do not know, but we know they did come seeking Him. First they came to Jerusalem and then at last to Bethlehem, following the star. Again, we know nothing of the exact nature of that star, but we do know from the three leading Roman historians of that same era that there was widespread belief all over the far-flung empire that a great deliverer king would come from Judea. This may account for the ferocity of the Roman suppression of the Jews. But the wise men came voicing the hopes and longings of their own hearts and that of millions of people: "Where is He who is born King of the Jews? For we have seen His star in the east and are come to worship Him."

III. The Wise Men's Quest for Truth and Meaning

What an amazing admission on their part. They had searched for truth and meaning in every field of human inquiry and endeavor. They had studied science and were far advanced over their Roman and Western counterparts. Their knowledge of astronomy was amazing. In medicine, they were literally centuries ahead of their time. They were philosophers and thinkers, and had studied the various religions of their own world and time. Obviously, they had not found that for which they diligently sought: truth and meaning.

At long last, following both a star and the truths Daniel had left behind, they came to the least likely place in all the world where one might find truth and meaning. But they came wisely, and humbly, and in a spirit of worship as well as of seeking. What noble scholars, admitting their own failure and inability to discover the meaning to life and the ultimate truth, but still believing these things may be found. They had sought in every place to find these things, just as so many today still seek. The wise men had used their great learning and wisdom all to no avail. If there was an answer, it would be found only in the true and living God coming into this world in such a way that the gates of truth and meaning could be opened to seeking hearts. The wisdom they sought comes not from the ingenious mind of fallen man, but only from God as He is pleased to reveal Himself.

How could these things be found in a baby boy of peasant parents, and how would they know that at long last they had found ultimate wisdom and meaning? Perhaps the best answer to this is that God who led them on their long journey and protected them from the perils of travel over many a dangerous mile, had also protected their minds and hearts from more dangerous perils of a misguided search until He was pleased to show them the truth in his Son, and testified to their hearts that their search at long last was over.

I do know when they found Him, they worshiped Him and gave Him their costly gifts. But He gave to them their hearts' desires. For in Him, they found the true God, the great promised King, and a Savior; for these are the things represented by the treasures they laid at His feet.

Where is your search for truth, wisdom, and meaning taking you? If it does not lead you to Bethlehem, and the truth that God was in Christ, saving, forgiving, and regenerating you, then you will look in vain into all the black holes of pride and folly with which the wisdom of the world tempts you every day, and in the end you will never see the Kingdom of God. So come humbly, lovingly, and join with the wise men of old to worship Him who is the true King and only Savior.

As with Gladness Men of Old

Words: William Chatterton Dix (1837-1898), 1860
Music: Melody, Conrad Kocher (1786-1872), 1838; arr., William Henry Monk (1823-1889), 1861

Tune: *Dix*

Hymn Notes

This Epiphany hymn by William Chatterton Dix invites us to consider our own journey of faith through the example of the three wise men. Dix wrote it on January 6, 1860 while he was in the midst of recovering from a long illness. He once reported that he began writing the hymn after reading the Gospel passage assigned to that day. January 6 is the Feast of the Epiphany — the day set aside in liturgical churches to recall the visit of the wise men to the Christ Child. Thus, the Gospel reading for that day would have been Matthew 2:1-12.

In a letter written to Francis Arthur Jones in 1900, Dix described the hymn's creation. Mr. Jones discussed that letter in his book, *Famous Hymns and Their Authors*:

> In a letter received from the author shortly before his lamented death in 1900, Mr. Dix informed me that there was little of interest to record respecting its composition. He was unwell at the time, slowly recovering from a rather serious illness. One evening, when he felt somewhat stronger than he had for several days, the lines of the now well-known hymn gradually formed themselves in his brain, and, asking for writing materials, he committed them to paper. The following year it was published in a small hymnal, which had a very limited circulation. From thence it made its way into more popular collections, and today its reputation has become worldwide.
>
> *- Francis Arthur Jones, Famous Hymns and Their Authors,*
> *Hodder and Stoughton, 1903, pp. 63-64*

As with gladness men of old is structured as a prayer. In the first three stanzas, the "as they … so may we" pattern draws attention to the faithful actions of the magi and concludes with a prayer that we might conduct our own life journeys with similar faithfulness. The first stanza is a prayer for guidance, the second for a heart to seek that grace, and the third for willingness to offer Christ our most cherished gift of love. The last two stanzas complete the prayer for faithfulness in our earthly journey, that we may be guided to fullness of life in the Kingdom of God.

The hymn's first publication occurred in *Hymns for Public Worship and Private Devotion* (1860). The following year, it was published in Dix's *Hymns of Love and Joy* and in *Hymns Ancient and Modern*. Since then, it has been included in almost every hymnal in English-speaking countries.

William C. Dix was born in 1837 in Bristol, England. His father was a surgeon and an author. William Dix was one of a handful of 19th century hymn writers who was not a clergyman. Dix was a business man who spent the better part of his career managing a marine insurance company in Glasgow, Scotland. He published several volumes of hymns, a number of which were selected for inclusion in the authoritative *Hymns Ancient and Modern*. In addition to *As with gladness men of old*, familiar among the list of titles are *What child is this* and *Alleluia, sing to Jesus*.

The hymn's tune passed through the hands of two musicians before it reached completion. The first was German composer and church musician Conrad Kocher, who adapted a melody he had written in 1838 for a chorale, *Treuer Heiland, wir sind hier* (*Faithful Savior, we are here*). The second was William H. Monk, organist and professor of vocal music at King's College, Cambridge, and music editor of the first edition of *Hymns Ancient and Modern*. Before its publication in that esteemed hymnal, Monk altered the tune further to better fit the poetic meter of *As with gladness, men of old*. It has been written that Dix did not like the tune. Nevertheless, it was judged to be such a good match that the tune was named for him. The hymn is never sung to any other tune.

- TW

A Letter, The Ninth Lesson, and a Carol

Presentation in the Temple, ca. 1470/1480

Master of the Prado (15th century), Netherlands

Oil on panel

National Gallery of Art Open Access Image

This artist's identity has been long lost. He is believed to have been a student of Rogier van der Weyden (1400-1464) because his work bears a strong similarity to that of van der Weyden. The artist is named for a masterful copy that he made of van der Weyden's "The Adoration of the Magi," a panel from the older artist's *St. Columba Altarpiece*.

Celebrating Advent 2015

Dearly Beloved,

Christmas is the time to reflect upon the good news of God's redeeming love for mankind. From the very beginning of the Gospel, we hear again and again of this good news. When the angel Gabriel came to God's priest, Zacharias, in the temple to announce the birth of John the Baptist, he came with these words: "Your wife Elizabeth will bear you a son, and you will give him the name John. You will have joy and gladness, and many will rejoice at his birth." When Zacharias expressed doubt, since both he and his wife were well beyond childbearing years, Gabriel responded, "… I have been sent by God to bring you this good news." Later, Gabriel was sent to the Virgin Mary, to tell her even better news: She was chosen to be the mother of the Messiah. After the birth of Jesus, the angel (presumably Gabriel) appeared to the shepherds saying, "I bring you good news of great joy …"

So even today, Christmas remains the best of good news. How we need that good news! We need it because without it we would be eternally lost. We need it because in this world we are bombarded with bad news all the time. We need it because we have been called and commissioned to be heralds of the Kingdom, bringing to all people everywhere the great and glorious news that in the birth of Jesus, "God was in Christ, reconciling the world unto Himself." The news is good because it comes from God. It is good because it is true. It is good because it alone meets the deepest needs and longings of all people. It is good because to believe it brings salvation, hope, and heaven. And that's good!

May you have a joyful and good Christmas, and may God's grace and love rest on you and all those you love.

With sincere love and many prayers,

Gordon and Miriam Reed

The Sword that Broke Mary's Heart
A Christmas Eve Communion Meditation

> Now there was a man in Jerusalem, whose name was Simeon, and this man was righteous and devout, waiting for the consolation of Israel, and the Holy Spirit was upon him. ²⁶ And it had been revealed to him by the Holy Spirit that he would not see death before he had seen the Lord's Christ. ²⁷ And he came in the Spirit into the temple, and when the parents brought in the child Jesus, to do for him according to the custom of the Law, ²⁸ he took him up in his arms and blessed God and said, ²⁹ "Lord, now you are letting your servant depart in peace, according to your word; ³⁰ for my eyes have seen your salvation ³¹ that you have prepared in the presence of all peoples, ³² a light for revelation to the Gentiles, and for glory to your people Israel." ³³ And his father and his mother marveled at what was said about him. ³⁴ And Simeon blessed them and said to Mary his mother, "Behold, this child is appointed for the fall and rising of many in Israel, and for a sign that is opposed ³⁵ (and a sword will pierce through your own soul also), so that thoughts from many hearts may be revealed." ³⁶ And there was a prophetess, Anna, the daughter of Phanuel, of the tribe of Asher. She was advanced in years, having lived with her husband seven years from when she was a virgin, ³⁷ and then as a widow until she was eighty-four. She did not depart from the temple, worshiping with fasting and prayer night and day. ³⁸ And coming up at that very hour she began to give thanks to God and to speak of him to all who were waiting for the redemption of Jerusalem.
>
> *- Luke 2:25-38*

What a shocking surprise awaited Mary when she and Joseph took the infant Jesus to the temple to present Him to the Lord as required by the law of Moses, and to offer the necessary sacrifices both for Him and for Mary. The unwanted surprise came from the lips of an aged saint named Simeon. But before we consider his words to Mary concerning her baby, let's go back and listen to everything that had been said about Him up to this point.

When the angel Gabriel was sent by God to bring Mary the startling announcement that she had been chosen as mother of the Messiah, he told her some truly amazing things about Him. First, His conception would be by the Holy Spirit and not by ordinary human processes. Now listen to Gabriel's description of this coming miraculous baby: "Behold, you will conceive in your womb and bring forth a Son and shall call His name Jesus. He will be great, and will be called the Son of the Most High: And the Lord God will give Him the throne of His father, David. And He will reign over the house of Jacob forever, and of His kingdom there will be no end." Is there contained in these words even a hint of suffering?

But that's not all. Her cousin Elizabeth was so overwhelmingly joyful when Mary came to see her. Her song of praise to God and Mary's Magnificat were both hymns of praise that at long last the Messiah was now coming with power and victory over Israel's enemies. Remember the visit from the shepherds? They told Mary and Joseph and everyone else who would listen what the angels had told them as they were keeping watch over their flocks by night. God was giving them a Savior, Christ the Lord, yet born in lowly surroundings just as if He were a poor shepherd's child. And Mary kept all these things and pondered them in her heart.

We really don't know how the timing of the visit from the wise men fitted into this whole scenario, but their gifts of gold, frankincense, and myrrh were presented to the young Jesus only after they had fallen on their knees before Him and worshiped Him. They found the King of the Jews in this little child.

Now back to the service of dedication in the temple and the words of old Simeon concerning this baby whom he took in his arms and began to praise God for sending His salvation, which He had promised Simeon he would see before he died. Listen again to those words: "Now, Lord, you are letting your servant depart in peace according to your word; for my eyes have seen your salvation, which You prepared before the face of all people; a light to bring revelation to the Gentiles, and the glory of Your people Israel." The aged widow Anna, who served God in the temple night and day, also found hope in the infant Jesus and looked for the salvation He would bring to God's people.

So you see, Mary (and Joseph) had been told of the glory of His advent, and given assurance that it was He, their baby boy, who would save His people. "Mary and Joseph marveled at all those things which were spoken of Him."

Now come these strange words from the same old man who joined them in rejoicing over the baby Jesus, the true Messiah. He spoke these words to Mary: "Behold, this child is destined for the fall and rising of many in Israel, and for a sign which will be spoken against, and yes a sword will pierce through your own soul also." What a strange thing to say of the great Messiah King, God's Son who had come to save His people and to reign over the Kingdom of God forever.

What a dissonant note in the heavenly and earthly music of praise which had fallen on the ears of Mary. How strange and yet how true, for these words spoken by Simeon are the reason we gather on Christmas Eve and come to the table of our Lord to remember not just His birth, but also His death.

I sometimes call this the hidden message of Christmas for, truly, the best of the good news for many lies buried under the tinsel of the superficial celebration of

Christmas in which millions join, both believers and unbelievers alike.

Simeon's words reveal that the coming of Christ would be a time of decision and of judgment. Later, as His earthly ministry was drawing to an end, He said these words about Himself and His mission: "For judgment I have come into this world." In John's Gospel, we read: "This is the condemnation, that Light has come into the world, and men loved darkness rather than Light."

So, the child who was ushered into the world with angels' song, adored by shepherds, worshiped by wise men, and hailed by Anna and Simeon as the Lord's Messiah, was also destined to be despised and rejected by man, a man of sorrows and acquainted with grief; scorned, mocked, hated, beaten, betrayed, murdered. Yes, He came to save sinners, but Himself He could not save. It was only a few miles from Bethlehem's manger to Calvary's cross, but that path became the road of destiny for all people, for all who meet Him on that pathway are faced with the ultimate decision and judgment.

The coming of Christ into the world created a crisis for all people. Believe Him, accept His word, trust in His grace, and find life eternal and abundant. Reject Him, or even try to ignore Him or attempt to be neutral about Him, and invite judgment, wrath, and death upon yourself.

We celebrate both nativity and Calvary at this table tonight. The two cannot be separated, not even for Christmas Day. We are here to rejoice in our Savior's birth and also His atoning death, but even more in the victory He has won for us and the great hope of his glorious return. Like Simeon, we know this Child is destined for the fall and rising again of many. Like Anna, by faith we see a glory on the horizon of the future. Poor faithful, gentle Mary had no idea at that moment that Simeon's words foretold a gathering storm of disappointment, pain, and sorrow beyond all words. Maybe she thought of those words of warning as shortly thereafter the Holy Family fled the wrath and terror of Herod. Perhaps they came back to her mind when her oldest son left home and began His public ministry. No doubt she was thrilled to know of His miracles of grace and healing, but troubled by the increasing opposition and even hatred of the rulers. Then came that day which burned itself into her memory and ours forever. The sword of which Simeon had warned broke her heart. On that day, she saw Him staggering under the weight of the cross He bore to Calvary's hill. She saw the terrible wounds caused by the lashing He endured. She saw Him nailed to that bitter tree and lifted up to suffer and to die before a mocking multitude. On that dreadful day, the sun was darkened, the earth was rent with a mighty earthquake, and from the cross a cry went up, "My God, my God, why hast Thou forsaken me?"

Yes, on that day Mary's beloved Son, so recently only a baby at her breast and a little boy dancing and singing with joy on His way to the temple, died on that lonely hill. The one we call "Wonderful Counselor, Mighty God, Everlasting Father, Prince of Peace," was also "the Lamb of God who takes away the sin of the world." The Prince of Peace was robbed of peace, that we might know the highest joy and peace of sins forgiven and life eternal.

By coming to this table tonight of all nights, we are renewing our vows, taking our stand, repenting of our sins, and thus we have discovered what Christmas is really all about: the coming of our Savior who by His broken heart has mended ours.

Mary's broken heart has been forever healed. All her tears have been wiped away, and she is in that multitude who worship before the throne. And you may join her there one day with your broken heart healed, all your tears wiped away, and be filled with joy unspeakable forever and ever. And He will eat this bread and drink anew this cup in the Father's Kingdom, and we will join Him in that feast and in that Kingdom forever and ever. Amen.

Let All Mortal Flesh Keep Silence

1. Let all mortal flesh keep silence, and with fear and trembling stand; ponder nothing earthly minded, for with blessing in his hand, Christ our God to
2. King of kings, yet born of Mary, as of old on earth he stood, Lord of lords, in human vesture, in the body and the blood, he will give to
3. Rank on rank the host of heaven spreads its vanguard on the way, as the Light of light descendeth from the realms of endless day,
4. At his feet the six-winged seraph; cherubim, with sleepless eye, veil their faces to the presence, as with ceaseless voice they cry, "Alleluia,

Words: *Liturgy of St. James*, 5th century; adapted Gerard Moultrie (1829-1885), 1864
Music: French melody, 17th century; arr. Ralph Vaughan Williams (1872-1958), 1906

Tune: *Picardy*

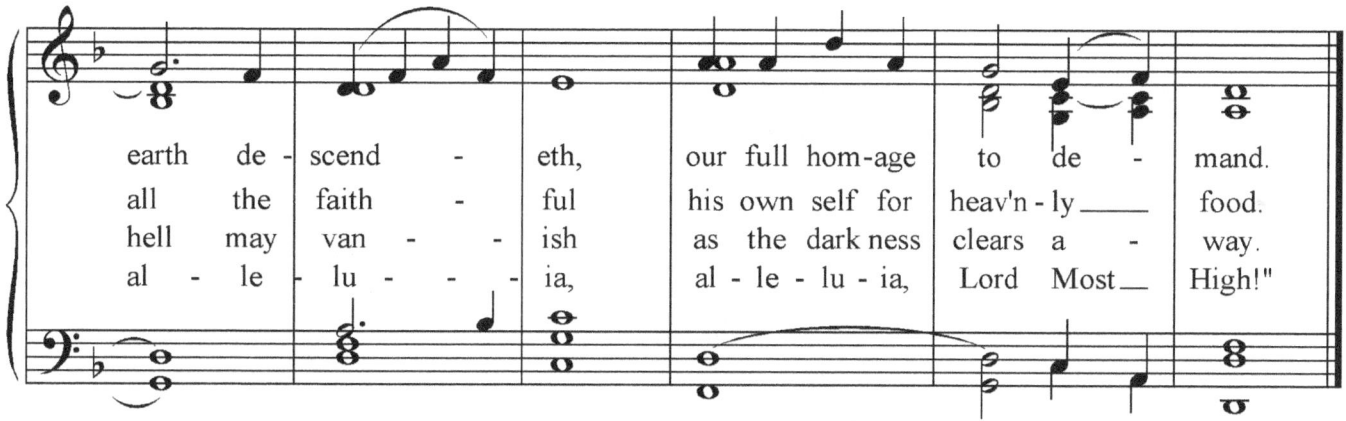

Hymn Notes

This 19th century Advent and Christmas hymn is based on a Greek text that connects us to the Liturgy of Saint James, a form of Christian worship that has been in continuous use for over 1,600 years. It remains in use today in the Eastern Orthodox Church. Scholars argue over the authorship of the liturgy. Some associate it with a prayer written in 60 A.D. by James the Less, one of the twelve apostles. Others ascribe it to Cyril of Jerusalem. Whatever the source of its elements may be, there is no doubt that the Liturgy of St. James was developed for use in the Church at Jerusalem near the end of the fourth century. By the early part of the fifth century, it was the primary liturgy of the churches at Jerusalem and Antioch.

In its structure, the worship service begins with scripture readings, prayers, and hymns, and culminates with the Lord's Supper. At the beginning of the Lord's Supper, the priest chants a prayer called the Cherubic Hymn:

> We remember the sky, the earth and the sea, the sun and the moon, the stars and all creation both rational and irrational, the angels and archangels, powers, mights, dominations, principalities, thrones, the many-eyed Cherubim who also say those words of David: 'Praise the Lord with me.' We remember also the Seraphim, whom Isaiah saw in spirit standing around the throne of God, who with two wings cover their faces, with two their feet and with two fly; who say: 'Holy, holy, holy, Lord of Sabaoth.' We also say these divine words of the Seraphim, so as to take part in the hymns of the heavenly host.

In 1864, Gerard Moultrie translated this text from its original Greek, paraphrased it, and published it as *Prayer of the Cherubic Hymn.* We know it as *Let All Mortal Flesh Keep Silence*.

The ancient Greek text served as a Eucharistic hymn that reflected upon the mystery of the Lord's Supper and the reality that all creation joins with us around the Lord's table. Moultrie's paraphrase stretches beyond that to invite reflection upon the glory of Christ and the mystery of His Incarnation. It asks us to marvel at the nature of His birth: the King of kings, born on earth of a lowly maiden. It bids us to join the ranks of angels in unceasing, deafening cries of praise to Christ. Lastly, it paints Christ's birth with a majesty and sense of awe that transcends the event at Bethlehem. Consider the text in light of Isaiah's vision as recorded in Isaiah 6, as well as John's vision in Revelation 4.

The tune to which the hymn is set is a 17th century French carol. The renowned composer Ralph Vaughan Williams paired it with Moultrie's text for publication in the *English Hymnal* in 1906. It is the only tune that has ever been paired with this hymn. Perhaps the reason for that rests in its minor key, which seems to perfectly express the wonder and majesty that the text communicates.

South Carolinians, and indeed anyone interested in the Revolutionary War, might wonder if there is a connection between Gerard Moultrie and the South Carolina Moultries. Yes! Gerard Moultrie's great-grandfather was a South Carolina Loyalist who moved to England at the outbreak of the Revolutionary War. His great-granduncle was William Moultrie, a General in the Continental Army and then Governor of South Carolina (1785-1787 and 1792-1794). Gerard was born in Bristol, England and, like his father, the Rev. John Moultrie, grew up to become an Anglican priest and a poet. His works were published in seven volumes. His small body of hymns - numbering about 30 - includes translations from Greek, Latin, and German hymns.   *- TW*

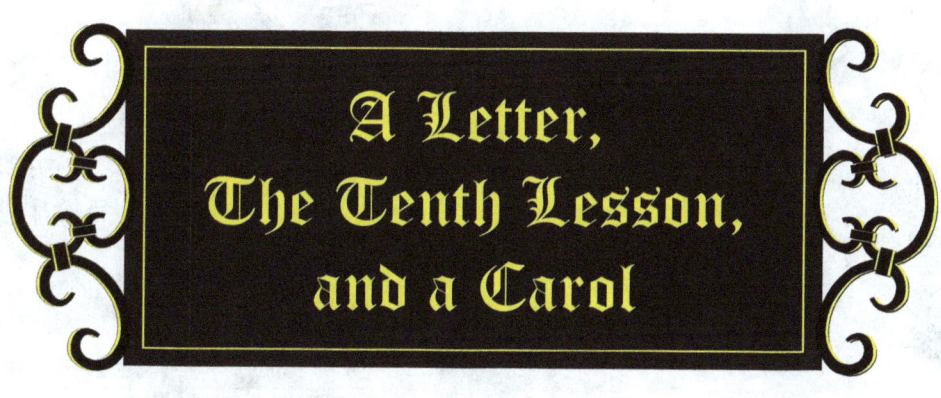

The Adoration of the Shepherds and the Magi, 1846

Stained Glass Window, Cologne Cathedral (Germany)
Creative Commons via Wikimedia Commons (CC BY-2.0)

This work of stained glass art is a glorious rendition of salvation history. Although cut off in this image, we can just see at the top of the window, moving from left to right: a representation of the Fall through the images of Adam, Eve, and the serpent; the Annunciation to Mary; and an image of Mary standing on a dragon as a symbol of her victory over sin, and holding a lily in her hand as a symbol of her virginity. The central scene combines the adoration of the shepherds and the adoration of the magi, with angels hovering above. Unseen in this reduced photograph of the window, the four major prophets who foretold the coming of the Messiah - Isaiah, Jeremiah, Ezekiel, and Daniel - are depicted in its lower portion.

Tucked away in the lower right and left corners is acknowledgement of the window's donor, King Ludwig I. Look closely to see the Bavarian coat of arms and donation inscription (dated 1846). The window was installed in 1848 as part of the celebrations marking the 600th anniversary of the start of construction on the cathedral.

The Comfort of Christmas

A Devotional for Christmas Eve or Christmas Day

Dearly Beloved,

Very early on Christmas Day, many years ago, I received a telephone call. There was really nothing unusual about getting a call so early in the morning, especially on Christmas Day. I had many friends and family members who called me to wish me a merry and blessed Christmas. This call was different from the rest. When I answered that call, as was my custom on Christmas Day, I said, "Merry Christmas, God bless you." The call came from a nephew named Danny. "Uncle Gordon," he began, "Daddy is celebrating Christmas with Jesus in heaven today." To say the least, that was not what I expected from my first Christmas call that year. Danny went on to explain that his daddy, my brother-in-law, had suffered a massive heart attack late the night before and died right then and there with his family around him, assuring him of their great love for him and telling him goodbye 'til we meet in heaven.

When my sister came on the phone, she was obviously sad and upset, but amazingly calm and obviously at peace. (She is truly at peace now for she, too, is with the Lord in heaven.) After she heard me in my clumsy way telling her my feeling of grief and loss, and assuring her of my sympathy, love, and prayers, she simply said, "What better place than heaven, with the Lord, for Dan to celebrate Christmas." She said her first reaction when she realized Dan was dying was, "Please Lord, not on Christmas Eve!" Her next thought was, "But isn't this truly what Christmas is all about, that because of Christmas God has defeated death by sending His Son into the world?" So, she quieted her own heart and the hearts of her children gathered around her, and they prayed together.

The first words in Isaiah 40 are these: "Comfort, yes comfort my people says your God. Speak comfort to Jerusalem, and cry out to her, that her warfare is ended, that her iniquity is pardoned." It seems to me this is really an explanation of what Christmas means. It is a message of comfort, for it tells us that our sins have been forgiven, and we have peace with God through our Lord Jesus Christ. But Christmas points us to another event, or should I say 'advent'. The message of comfort which Christmas brings is not complete without the good news that our Lord is coming again, and that He has opened heaven to His people.

Yes, the sorrows of this life are real and many. We are reminded at Christmas of the loss of loved ones, whether recently or in days gone by, and our grief is renewed and the heart wounds are reopened and the pain returns. But God has a message of comfort, peace, and hope. We sorrow not as others who have no hope. We anticipate, yes, we long for that blessed day when we shall meet our loved ones again and will never again be separated from them. Until that day, hear God saying in His word, "Comfort, yes comfort my people … For those who wait upon the Lord shall renew their strength. They shall mount up with wings like eagles. They shall run and not be weary, they shall walk and not faint."

Our loving prayers are with you all. "The Lord bless you and keep you. The Lord make His face to sine upon you and be gracious unto you. The Lord lift up His countenance upon you and give you peace." This Christmas and forever.

With sincere love and many prayers,

Gordon and Miriam Reed

The Last Christmas Will Last Forever

> LORD, you are my God; I will exalt you; I will praise your name, for you have done wonderful things, plans formed of old, faithful and sure. ² For you have made the city a heap, the fortified city a ruin; the foreigners' palace is a city no more; it will never be rebuilt. ³ Therefore strong peoples will glorify you; cities of ruthless nations will fear you. ⁴ For you have been a stronghold to the poor, a stronghold to the needy in his distress, a shelter from the storm and a shade from the heat; for the breath of the ruthless is like a storm against a wall, ⁵ like heat in a dry place. You subdue the noise of the foreigners; as heat by the shade of a cloud, so the song of the ruthless is put down. ⁶ On this mountain the LORD of hosts will make for all peoples a feast of rich food, a feast of well-aged wine, of rich food full of marrow, of aged wine well refined. ⁷ And he will swallow up on this mountain the covering that is cast over all peoples, the veil that is spread over all nations. ⁸ He will swallow up death forever; and the Lord GOD will wipe away tears from all faces, and the reproach of his people he will take away from all the earth, for the LORD has spoken. ⁹ It will be said on that day, "Behold, this is our God; we have waited for him, that he might save us. This is the LORD; we have waited for him; let us be glad and rejoice in his salvation." ¹⁰ For the hand of the LORD will rest on this mountain, and Moab shall be trampled down in his place, as straw is trampled down in a dunghill. ¹¹ And he will spread out his hands in the midst of it as a swimmer spreads his hands out to swim, but the LORD will lay low his pompous pride together with the skill of his hands. ¹² And the high fortifications of his walls he will bring down, lay low, and cast to the ground, to the dust.
>
> - Isaiah 25

Everyone on earth who has ever celebrated Christmas will one day celebrate their last earthly Christmas. That means me and you. Even as we gather today on this last Sunday in Advent to rejoice in our Savior's birth and to look back one last time on Christmas Day, we recognize that there were some with us this time last year who have gone on to be with the Lord.

But for us, too, there will come a Christmas which will be our last ever on earth. This adds a note of seriousness and even sorrow, for we know we simply cannot hold on to any earthly joys forever; they slip away with the passing of years. One day, there will come a very last Christmas for the entire world.

BUT!!

"Behold, I bring you good tidings of great joy" in the midst of this sobering reminder. The Lord, who came so long ago, will come again, and the joy experienced by Joseph, Mary, the shepherds, and the wise men, will be as nothing compared to the joy of that day. For when he comes again, Christmas will at last be fulfilled and will last forever and ever. Even the most exciting Christmas you have ever known cannot match the thrill, the wonder, and the joy of that forever Christmas which is coming. Simon Peter said, "But according to His promise, we are looking for new heavens and a new earth in which righteousness lives." Paul said in Romans 8: "For I consider the sufferings of this present time are not worth comparing to the glory that is to be revealed to us. For Creation waits eagerly for the full revealing of the sons of God … that the creation itself will be set free from the bondage to decay and obtain the freedom of the glory of God's children." Jesus said, "Behold I make all things new!"

My point is that what makes Christmas so very exciting is not the presents, parties, decorating our homes and yards, and seeing friends and family — as much as we enjoy these things — but the real joy and trembling excitement really comes from anticipating what will finally unfold of God's Christmas present to us: a new creation, a renewed world, far more glorious and real than this present wonderful world, in which real, resurrected people will be reunited once more and then forever. I long to see my mother and daddy again and thank them for all the wonderful Christmases they gave me when I was a little boy growing up in a time of poverty. I was not even aware of how poor we were because of their sacrificial love for me.

I can still remember several Christmases of long ago. I remember that unbelievable Christmas when Aunt Dobby sent me a wind-up toy train, and Mother and Daddy gave me a great big red wagon; two great toys on the same Christmas! That Christmas was far more wonderful than anything I had ever imagined it could possibly be. I remember the Christmas Eve as a teenager, slightly cynical by that time, when after the Christmas pageant was over — in which I was the wise man who sang, "myrrh is mine its bitter perfume …" (I think my singing must have been pretty "bitter perfume" to all who heard it) — we walked outside to go home and a sudden and unexpected snowstorm was swirling all around us. There was a sense of the closeness of the Lord and the reality of the Incarnation such as I had never known before. Then, best of all, I remember that Christmas many years ago when I had my first date with Miriam, and we both knew immediately this was for "as long as we both shall live" — truly the best Christmas present ever.

Yet I had no idea how wonderful life with Miriam would be. And of course, and as a result of that Christmas, a whole bunch of merry and exciting Christmases with five little Reeds followed right along. But even all these thrilling Christmases have passed into sweet and blessed memory.

Again, what is my point? Just this: When at last we enter the New Creation, it will far exceed anything we might imagine now. So, now let me tell you of that last

Christmas which will last forever, and not just in sweet memory. I assure you it will exceed anything we ever imagined life in the New Creation could possibly be.

I. The Setting for this Amazing Prophecy

Isaiah had the sad duty to tell Judah of her coming destruction and of the approaching Babylonian captivity. Even God's holy temple would be destroyed. But God mitigated his sorrow and the fears of the Jews by also revealing to Isaiah that there would come a time when the captives would return and rebuild the city and the temple.

Using the imagery of the captives returning and the great joy over their release, Isaiah foretold of a far greater victory of God over all His and our enemies. He saw a time in the distant future when God would reign over all His people in a perfect and never-ending kingdom of peace. All His foes would be destroyed; even death will fall victim to His great power, and in that glory kingdom we will say, "There will be no more death."

II. The Anthem of Joy

The prophet begins by singing the faithfulness and power of God: "O Lord, you are my God. I will exalt you. I will praise your name, for You have done wonderful things; Your counsels of old are faithful and true." Everything we believe as Christians is based on our faith and confidence in the greatness and goodness of our Heavenly Father. We sing of Him, "Great is thy faithfulness." God has proven Himself to be the faithful and trustworthy Lord, whose word is true and whose promises are sure. We believe, therefore, that God will bring to pass all His great promises, even the end of death, because He has shown His great power in so many ways. He has revealed Himself both in judgment and mercy. Isaiah saw in the ruin of nations which had exalted themselves against God, the sure proof of God's righteousness and His power. Yes, even in the captivity of His own people, God displayed His faithfulness and His righteousness.

But even more, the goodness of God was clearly seen, too. Listen: "You have been a strength to the poor, and to the needy in his distress. A refuge from the storm, a shade from the heat…" In the midst of life's sorrows, in the crucible of the fiery trials of faith, of perplexing doubts and unanswered questions, God comes to His people and gives them the strength and comfort of His dear presence. We find our refuge in the Rock of Ages. We find our healing in the hands of the Great Physician. We find renewed strength as we feed on the Bread of Life. All Scripture and all our experiences in life combine to teach us that God is true and faithful, and His promises will not fail.

But there looms in the dark background of Isaiah's vision a sobering truth. God's great and final victory is to be preceded by a time of great suffering and terrible disaster. In Matthew 24, Jesus fills in the picture in words of terrifying proportions, surpassing all the natural disasters the world has ever seen. In Isaiah's time, the coming disaster could be seen in the near future of Judah's destiny. The signs were unmistakable. Sin was rampant; unfaithfulness of the Chosen People abounded. Great powers of the world were arrayed against little Judah, and she had insulted and rejected her only true Defender and her only hope. Surely judgment would fall soon, and it did.

Even as Isaiah was not blind to the terrible prelude to the coming deliverance, so we must open our eyes, too. God is still the same righteous God who chastised his people with a terrible wrath. He rebukes evil wherever it is found. He still brings punishment on those who ignore His law and despise His grace. The judgment upon Judah is a mere example of an abiding principle, and a prophecy of that which will come upon the whole world. There will come a day of final judgment. Our great hope, the coming of Christ and His eternal kingdom, will not occur until that judgment first comes. "God has appointed a day when He will judge the world by Jesus Christ."

As we see history rushing towards its ultimate destiny, we see more and more not only the inevitability, but the need of God's purifying judgment. Our rainbow of hope is spread over a terrible storm. "Fear not, for behold I bring you good tidings of great joy … Unto you is born a Savior, Christ the Lord." Judgment is a necessary precursor to the supreme victory God will win at Christ's return. Here we find the heart and soul of what Christmas and Christianity are really all about. Hear these words: "God will destroy the face of covering cast over all people, and the veil spread over all nations. He will swallow up death in victory, and the Lord God will wipe away tears from off all faces …"

This means not only the end of death, but the end to what caused death … sin! God's ultimate purpose in His judgment is to destroy sin and its cursed consequences. He will lift the darkness and the curse which fell on mankind in the ruined Garden of Eden. When the human race fell that black day long ago, we traded away holiness and happiness for sinfulness and misery. What a miserable swap! The promise of this passage, and in fact of the New Testament as well, is that God will lift the curse, destroy the power of sin and death, and reclaim His violated creation. And behold, it will be very good!

It is difficult for us to really comprehend the greatness of this joy and what it will be like to live forever in a sin-free creation. There will be an end to all frustrations and failures, all disappointment in ourselves and others. There will be an end to loneliness, sorrow, and separation; an end to all hate, suspicion, mistrust, vile temper, and hateful designs. No more warfare between nations or within families, and, of course, there will be the death of death! Thus will end all rebuke and scorn of God's people. Listen to Isaiah's sunburst of joyful song: "And in that day it shall be said, lo! this is our God, we have waited for Him and He will save us: this is the Lord, we have waited for Him, we will be glad and rejoice in His salvation."

Now, leap ahead with me for a moment to that heavenly scene in Revelation 5, when for the first time all the redeemed from all generations and nations meet before the throne and unite in this joyful song: "Worthy is the Lamb who was slain and has redeemed us to God by His blood ... You have made us kings and priests to our God and we shall reign on the earth."

Such are the promises God has made to His precious elect, His beloved children. But where do you fit into this picture of grace and glory? What will be your role in this grand drama? Before you may be assured of your place in God's victorious Kingdom, you must experience His conquest of your heart and giving up control over your own life to Him. How do you do this? It begins with repentance, sincere and deeply felt. It includes faith in the Lord Jesus Christ as your Savior and Lord. Accepting God's great gift of salvation through His Son is very much like a little girl buying her daddy a Christmas present with the money he gave her to spend. And, of course, this experience of salvation goes on to include a lifetime of growing, changing, overcoming the habits and control of sin.

Would you like to take part in the very best Christmas ever, which lasts forever? Then come even now to Christ. Open the door of your heart that the King of Glory may come in. Then, one fine day, that same King of Glory will welcome you into the Kingdom and to the Christmas which will last forever.

> Then I saw a new heaven and a new earth, for the first heaven and the first earth had passed away, and the sea was no more. ² And I saw the holy city, new Jerusalem, coming down out of heaven from God, prepared as a bride adorned for her husband. ³ And I heard a loud voice from the throne saying, "Behold, the dwelling place of God is with man. He will dwell with them, and they will be his people, and God himself will be with them as their God. ⁴ He will wipe away every tear from their eyes, and death shall be no more, neither shall there be mourning, nor crying, nor pain anymore, for the former things have passed away." ⁵ And he who was seated on the throne said, "Behold, I am making all things new." Also he said, "Write this down, for these words are trustworthy and true." ⁶ And he said to me, "It is done! I am the Alpha and the Omega, the beginning and the end. To the thirsty I will give from the spring of the water of life without payment. ⁷ The one who conquers will have this heritage, and I will be his God and he will be my son. -
> *Revelation 21:1-7*

Hear it! Believe it!

Of the Father's Love Begotten

Words: Aurelius Clemens Prudentius (348-410); tr. John Mason Neale (1818-1866), 1854 and Henry Williams Baker (1821-1877), 1859
Music: Plainsong, ca. 11th century; adapt. *Piae Cantiones*, 1582

Tune: *Divinum mysterium*

Joy to the World

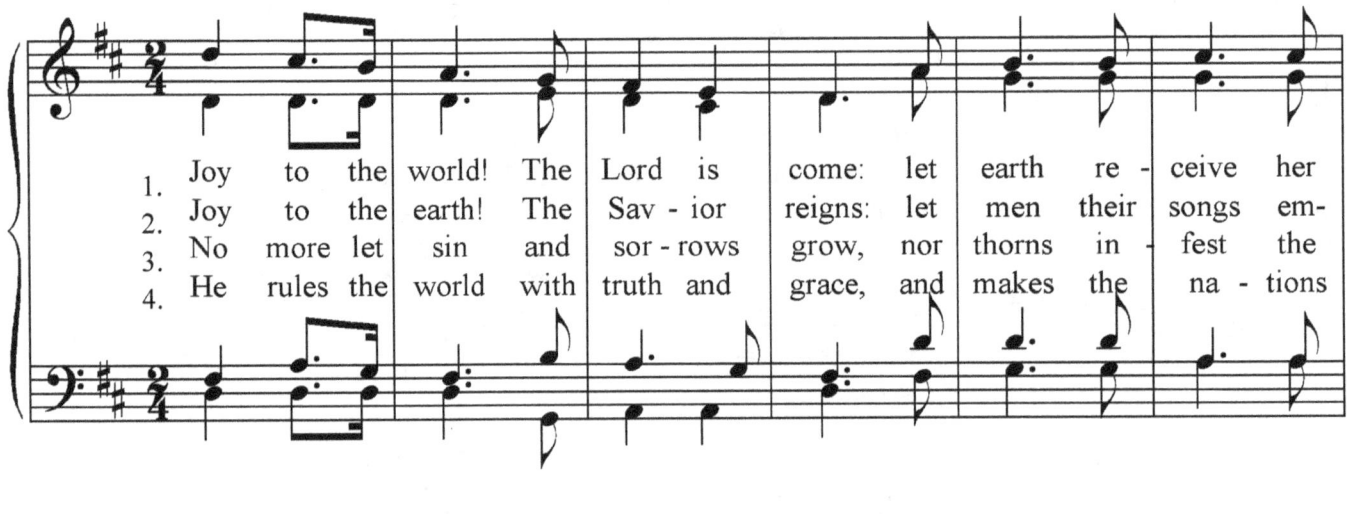

1. Joy to the world! The Lord is come: let earth receive her
2. Joy to the earth! The Savior reigns: let men their songs em-
3. No more let sin and sorrows grow, nor thorns infest the
4. He rules the world with truth and grace, and makes the nations

King; let ev-'ry heart prepare him room and
ply; while fields and floods, rocks, hills, and plains re-
ground; he comes to make his blessings flow far
prove the glories of his righteousness and

heav'n and nature sing, and heav'n and nature sing, and
peat the sounding joy, repeat the sounding joy, re-
as the curse is found, far as the curse is found, far
won - ders of his love, and won - ders of his love, and

Words: Isaac Watts (1674-1748), 1719; based on Psalm 98 and Genesis 3:17-18 (st. 3)
Music: Lowell Mason (1792-1872), 1848, after themes by George Frideric Handel (1665-1759)

Tune: *Antioch*

~ 168 ~

Hymn Notes

OF THE FATHER'S LOVE BEGOTTEN: Hymn historian Albert E. Bailey described this early fifth century hymn as a "fighting hymn."* Why? It was written in response to intense debates within the early Church over theological and doctrinal issues, largely the argument contesting the dual nature of Christ. The author, Marcus Aurelius Clemens Prudentius, was born in an era in which the Roman Empire was asserting its dominance, fighting and conquering the region but also bringing wealth and growth to those countries under its rule. Integral to all of this were the life and death struggles to spread Christianity itself: Those seeking its spread were up against those seeking with equal fervor to stop it.

All of this formed the backdrop against which Prudentius worked and wrote, but it was the theological debates among Christian leaders that directly informed his hymn-writing. One particularly lengthy and bitter debate developed over the nature of the Holy Trinity. The problem lay in a heresy - called Arianism - that stated that Christ is not divine but a created being. With the desire that the matter might finally be dealt with and resolved, the emperor Constantine called for a general council of the Church to be held at Nicaea (a town on the northwestern coast of Turkey, now called İznik). The First Council of Nicaea was held in 325. The council condemned the heretical teaching and affirmed that Jesus is indeed both human and divine, and of one nature with God. The Nicene Creed, a statement of faith used in all Christian churches, was the product of the council's discussions. It affirms that God the Father, God the Son, and God the Spirit are all of the same nature: one God in three persons. Although Prudentius was born 23 years after the Council of Nicaea, the conflicts referenced above continued to be part of the fabric of life, and the establishment and teaching of Christian doctrine was still raw. Prudentius felt it necessary to speak to the issues, and so wrote *Of the Father's love begotten* to underscore the affirmation of the Council as to Christ's nature. As he puts it, Christ was not made by God, but was "begotten" *of* the Father, and existed from before all time. The first stanzas of the hymn are rooted in the Messianic prophecies of Isaiah and Malachi, while the final two were inspired by John's vision as recorded in the Book of Revelation. It is because it addresses the Incarnation, from both divine and earthly perspectives (i.e. the virgin birth), that this hymn belongs to the Christmas season. Its relationship to the Book of Revelation and its cosmic undertones connect it to this chapter's lesson.

Prudentius wrote the hymn as part of a larger work, *Liber Cathemerinon* (roughly, *daily book*), consisting of twelve poems for personal devotion, one for each hour of the day. *Of the Father's love begotten* is comprised of verses from the ninth poem. The refrain "evermore and evermore" was not part of Prudentius' poem; it was added in the 11th century.

Prudentius, born in northern Spain in 348, is considered to be the most highly regarded Christian poet of his time. Through his writings, scholars have learned that he was a magistrate and served an appointment of some type at the imperial court in Rome. At age 57, for a reason that has not been clearly identified, Prudentius gave up his comfortable existence and took a vow to live the remainder of his life in poverty, devoting his time to meditation and writing. Albert Bailey noted that Prudentius "wrote 'to glorify God and atone for his sins,' to sing the praises of God, fight heresy, trample on heathen rites and celebrate the Apostles and martyrs."* All of his writings, even those dealing with theological matters, are presented in poetic form. *- TW*

Of the Father's love begotten was translated from Latin to English in 1854 by John Mason Neale. Neale ranks as one of the most gifted hymn translators in the history of western hymnody. His translations, together with those of John Wesley and Catherine Winkworth, enriched our body of hymnody in ways that cannot be measured. Of interest purely for its contrast to the views of so many other hymn writers, it is worth noting that Neale refused any personal claim to his work, stating that he was satisfied that his work be the "common property of Christendom."

In addition to his hymns and translations, Neale wrote many books on the subjects of liturgy and church history. His personal life was intensely complex. A poor summary of it would note that in spite of continual ill health, he devoted himself to service on behalf of those in need, developed a ministry to poor women and orphans, and founded the Sisterhood of St. Margaret, which grew to be considered among the best of religious training orders for nurses in England. He was an ordained priest in the Church of England but never served a parish, partly because of his health concerns but also because of his outspoken support of the Oxford Movement, a 19th century religious movement defined by Encyclopedia Britannica as a "movement centered at the University of Oxford that sought a renewal of Roman Catholic thought and practice within the Church of England in opposition to the Protestant tendencies of the church." Close on the heels, relatively speaking, of the tumultuous Protestant Reformation and tightly tied with both church and national politics, participants in the movement were not happily tolerated by the establishment.

The hymn's tune, known as *Divinum mysterium* (*divine mystery*), is a chant melody believed to date from the 10th century. It first appears in published form in *Piae Cantiones,* a 1582 Finnish collection of 74 sacred and secular church and school songs of medieval Europe compiled by Jaakko Suomalainenfrom. (See Hymn Notes, page 113.)

* *The Gospel in Hymns*, Albert E. Bailey, p. 223

JOY TO THE WORLD: There are two facts about this hymn that often come as a surprise. The first: It was not written as a Christmas hymn, nor is it based on the Christmas story. It is a paraphrase of Psalm 98 that focuses more on Christ's second coming than on His first. The second: The melody is not wholly taken from Handel's *Messiah*.

Taking the second point first, the fact is that the melody is a patchwork of snippets of melodies and rhythms from *Messiah*, combined with melodic fragments from other sources and alterations by several editors. For example, the first measure of the chorus, *Lift up your heads*, was adapted for the first four words of *Joy to the world*. The three-measure introduction to the recitative of the *Messiah* aria *Comfort ye* provides the idea for "and heaven and nature sing." This is the extent of Handel's contribution - or, more accurately, the extent of the "borrowing" of his work (a common practice in pre-copyright eras). Certainly the spirit of *Lift up your heads* permeates the carol, and the various arrangers of the melody created a fine whole out of assorted borrowed and cobbled parts.

An American had a hand in the development of the melody, too. Lowell Mason, an influential Boston music educator, is responsible for the music as we know it in the United States. He published his own arrangement in 1836 and named the tune *Antioch* after the city in Syria where believers were first called "Christians" (Acts 11:26).

Now as to the fact of the text. It is not based on the Christmas story. It is a paraphrase of Psalm 98. Isaac Watts, *Joy to the world's* paraphraser, was worthy of the title "Father of English Hymnody." His contributions to the body of Christian hymns cannot be underestimated. Of those contributions, one of prime importance was his ability to paraphrase psalms in such a way as to make them easily relatable to the average person. Hymnologist Albert E. Bailey describes it in this way: "He made David speak like King William III; England and Scotland take the place of Israel and Judah. Thus the Psalmist became 'an orthodox and patriotic English Christian of the early eighteenth century.'"** Watts took his work with the psalms to a level beyond that by rewriting them from a New Testament perspective. His treatment of Psalm 98 is no different. Quoting Bailey again, Watts "turns it into praise for the salvation of God's saints, a salvation that began when God became incarnate in the Babe of Bethlehem who was destined to remove the 'curse' entailed by Adam's fall. The old Jewish psalm thus became a Christian song of rejoicing, a Christmas carol. It is one of the most joyous Christmas hymns in existence; not in the sense of merry-making but in the deep and solemn realization of what Christ's birth has meant to mankind." ***

In an article about this carol, Dr. C. Michael Hawn considers all who contributed to its creation and sums it up in these words: "The result is a favorite Christmas hymn based on an Old Testament psalm, set to musical fragments composed in England, and pieced together across the Atlantic in the United States!"

**The Gospel in Hymns*, Albert E. Bailey, p. 49
***The Gospel in Hymns*, Albert E. Bailey, p. 54

Sources for Hymn Notes

Bailey, Albert Edward. *The Gospel in Hymns.* New York, New York: Charles Scribner's Sons, 1950.

Benson, Louis F. *Studies Of Familiar Hymns, First Series.* Philadelphia, PA: The Westminster Press, 1924

Editors of Encyclopædia Britannica, The. "Oxford Movement." Internet Encyclopaedia Britannica, www.britannica.com, 2017

Hawn, C. Michael. *History of Hymns: Joy to the World.* Discipleship Ministries, www.umcdiscipleship.org, 2017

Jones, Francis Arthur. *Famous Hymns and Their Authors.* London, England: Hodder and Stoughton, 1902.

Julian, John. *Dictionary of Hymnology.* London, England: John Murray, 1907 and New York, New York: Dover Publications, 1957 (reprint).

The Hymns and Carols of Christmas, www.hymnsandcarolsofchristmas.com, 1996.

www.hymnary.org

www.ingramcontent.com/pod-product-compliance
Lightning Source LLC
Chambersburg PA
CBHW080340170426
43194CB00014B/2634